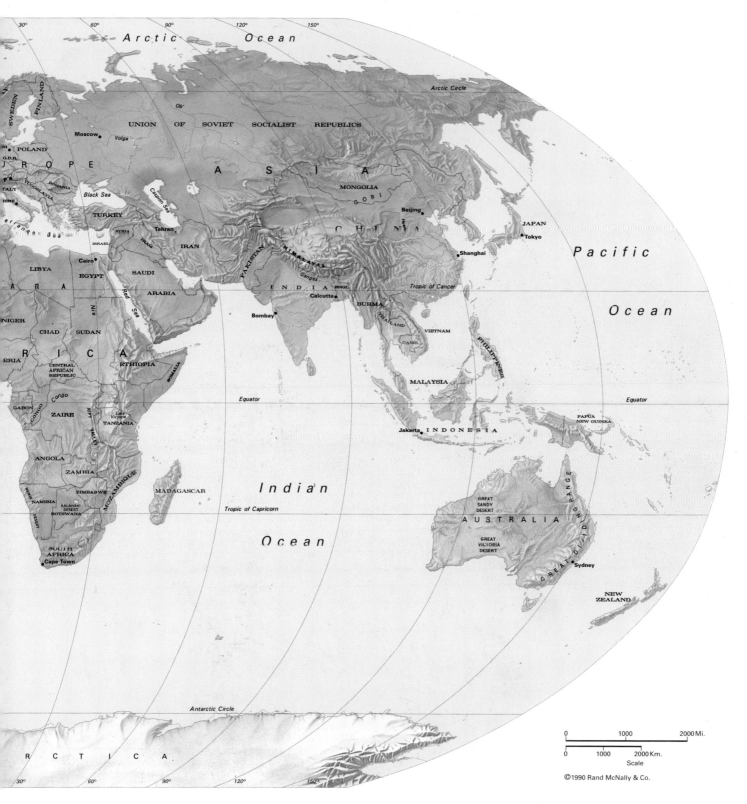

Rand McNally
Children's Atlas of
World
Wildlife

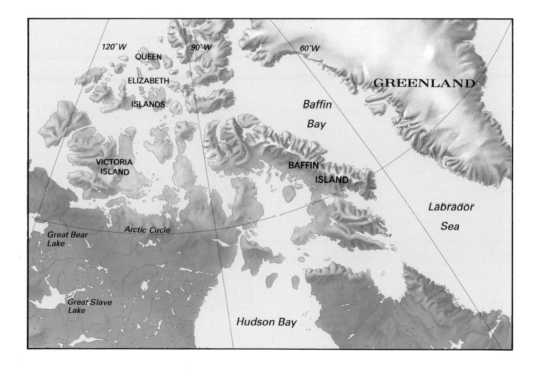

Rand McNally
Chicago • New York • San Francisco

Rand McNally Children's Atlas of World Wildlife

General manager: Russell L. Voisin
Managing editor: Jon M. Leverenz
Editor, writer: Elizabeth G. Fagan
Designer: Corasue Nicholas
Illustrator: Jan Wills
Production editor: Laura C. Schmidt
Production managers: John R. Potratz, Patricia Martin

Rand McNally Children's Atlas of World Wildlife
Copyright © 1990 by Rand McNally & Company

All photographs from Tom Stack & Associates as follows: Nancy Adams: 65 left. Rod Allin: 67 right, 77. Dominique Braud:
21 left, 23 left. John Cancalosi: 41 left, 46 left, 46 right, 47, 49 left, 49 right. W. Perry Conway: 53 right, 55 right. Buff &
Gerald Corsi: 69. Christopher Crowley: 68 left. Bill Everitt: 65 right. Dave B. Fleetham: 79 left. Jeff Foott: 33 top. Warren &
Genny Garst: 13 bottom, 33 bottom, 38 left, 54, 66-67. Susan Gibler: 23 right. Thomas Kitchin: 37 left, 53 left, 56. Sally
Lightfoot: 68 right. Larry Lipsky: 62 left. Joe McDonald: 26, 39, 57 right, 72. Gary Milburn: 17 left, 25, 29, 34, 35, 38 right,
41 right, 44, 48, 62 right. Mark Newman: 22, 24 right. Timothy O'Keefe: 17 right. Brian Parker: 14, 24 left, 28 left, 28 right,
36, 58, 59 left. Gary Randall: 37 right. Ed Robinson: 76 left, 76 right, 79 right. Leonard Lee Rue III: 12, 13 top, 15. Kevin
Schafer: 59 right, 63, 73 left. John Shaw: 32. Wendy Shattil & Robert Rozinski: 52. Richard P. Smith: 57 left. Diana L.
Stratton: 55 left. Dave Watts: 26-27, 45, 73 right. Robert Winslow: 21 right.

Library of Congress Catalog Card Number: 90-52621
ISBN: 0-528-83409-6

Contents

Introduction _____ 8

Europe map   **10**
Europe: Woodland _____ 12
Europe: Alpine _____ 14
Europe: Mediterranean _____ 16

Asia map   **18**
Asia: Northern Asia _____ 20
Asia: The Far East _____ 22
Asia: The Himalayas, Tibet,
     and Szechwan _____ 24
Asia: India _____ 26
Asia: Southeast Asia _____ 28

Africa and the Middle East map   **30**
Africa: Savanna _____ 32
Africa: Rain Forest _____ 34
Africa: Desert _____ 36
Africa: East Africa _____ 38
Africa: Madagascar _____ 40

Oceania map   **42**
Oceania: Tropical Australia and
     New Guinea _____ 44
Oceania: Arid Australia _____ 46
Oceania: Southeastern Australia,
     Tasmania, and New Zealand _____ 48

North America map   **50**
North America: Western
     Mountains _____ 52
North America: Great Plains _____ 54
North America: Eastern Forests
     and Swamps _____ 56
North America: Central America
     and the Caribbean _____ 58

South America map   **60**
South America: Rain Forest _____ 62
South America: Gran Chaco
     and Pampa _____ 64
South America: Andes _____ 66
South America: Galápagos Islands ___ 68

Polar Regions map   **70**
Polar Regions: The Arctic
     and Antarctica _____ 72

Oceans map   **74**
Oceans: Open Sea _____ 76
Oceans: Coral Reef _____ 78

Glossary _____ 80
Selected Threatened Animals _____ 82
Selected National Parks and
     Protected Areas _____ 84
Subject index _____ 87
Index to Major Places
     on the Maps _____ 90

Introduction

Do you know where wild grizzly bears live? Where can you find kangaroos in their natural habitat? And where do lions run free? An atlas answers the question "where?" This atlas shows where in the world to find wild animals like grizzly bears, kangaroos, lions, and hundreds of other types of wildlife.

Why Do Animals Live Where They Do?
The type and number of animals that live anywhere in the world depend on several factors. One factor is plant life, because animal life is dependent on plant life. Animals are part of a *food chain* or *food web*, at the bottom of which is plants. Plant-eating animals, called *herbivores*, are consumed by meat-eating animals, called *carnivores*. Carnivores are consumed by other carnivores, and so on.

Plant life varies according to natural forces such as climate. How hot or cold and how wet or dry a place is helps determine how many plants and what types of plants can grow there. In general, warmer, wetter places tend to have greater plant life. Because animal life is based on plant life, these places also tend to have a greater number and variety of animals than colder and drier places. Other factors such as altitude also affect plant life.

What Do the Large Maps Tell Us?
With the help of a *legend*, the large maps in this atlas can help you picture what a place is like. The different colors on the maps mean different types of *environments*. The legend shown below tells what the different colors mean. Notice that, on the maps, the environments gradually fade into neighboring environments, just like they do in the real world.

What Do the Lines on the Maps Mean?
The world's environments are affected by how far north and south they are. The North Pole and South Pole, the coldest areas, are the points around which the earth spins. The *equator* is an imaginary line midway between the poles that runs around the

Legend

Land Features

ICE AND SNOW

HIGH BARREN AREA

TUNDRA AND HIGH MOUNTAIN

CONIFEROUS FOREST

DECIDUOUS FOREST

TROPICAL RAIN FOREST

GRASSLAND

DRY SCRUB

DESERT

Water Features

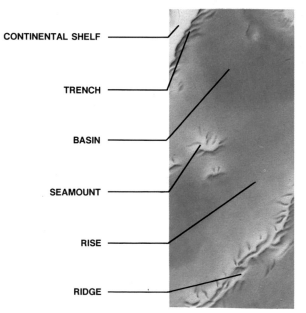
CONTINENTAL SHELF

TRENCH

BASIN

SEAMOUNT

RISE

RIDGE

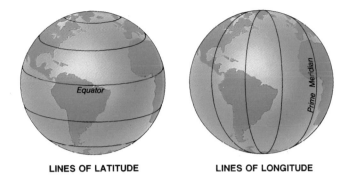

LINES OF LATITUDE   LINES OF LONGITUDE

earth and divides the planet into two parts. The regions along the equator are the hottest and wettest on earth.

The *Arctic Circle* is an imaginary line around the North Pole. North of the line, the sun does not shine for six months out of the year. The *Antarctic Circle* is the same kind of line, but it is around the South Pole. The climates within these circles tend to be bitterly cold much of the year.

The Tropic of Capricorn and the Tropic of Cancer are two more imaginary lines. The Tropic of Capricorn lies between the equator and the Antarctic Circle. The Tropic of Cancer is between the equator and the Arctic Circle. Between the two tropics is the *tropical* region of the earth. This region tends to have warm, wet—tropical—climates.

Between the tropics and the Arctic and Antarctic circles lie the *temperate* zones. These zones have generally moderate climates; that is, they lack long periods of extreme cold or heat. They also tend to have four distinct seasons.

Lines that run around the earth, such as the equator, are called lines of *latitude*, and they tell how far north or south a place is. In the diagram above, the lines of latitude shown are, from the top, the Arctic Circle, the Tropic of Cancer, the equator, the Tropic of Capricorn, and the Antarctic Circle. The other lines, the ones that run up and down, are called lines of *longitude*. They tell how far east or west a place is.

The distances determined by these lines are measured in *degrees*. Degrees of latitude are measured starting with zero at the equator. The numbers go higher as you travel north or south. Degrees of longitude begin with zero at the *prime meridian*, the line that goes through Greenwich, England. The numbers get higher as you travel east or west.

What Do the Small Maps Mean?

This atlas covers many, but not all, of the world's wildlife *habitats*, or places where a species or groups of species are found. Habitats are determined by such factors as temperature, moisture, and altitude. The small maps show the extent of the habitats of the animals under discussion. Because they locate the region of interest, these maps are called *locator maps*.

Locator Map

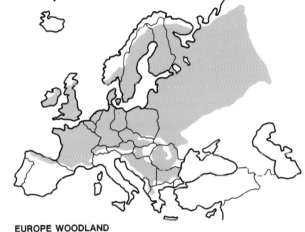

EUROPE WOODLAND

Some animals are found in several regions around the world. Other species wander far and wide in search of safe homes, food, and water and are sometimes found outside of their primary habitat. This book shows animals in their typical or usual habitats. These habitats are represented on the locator maps.

The habitats represented on the locator maps may not completely cover the area that is colored. In the European woodland section, for example, a large portion of Europe is colored in the locator. But forests do not cover the entire region. Much of the forest has been cut down by people. But where there are still forests within the colored region, the animals of woodland Europe might be found.

Europe

The great northern forests of Europe begin in Norway and extend into Sweden, Finland, and the Soviet Union. To the south of these forests is another belt of woodlands. It runs eastward between northern Spain and the United Kingdom, and all across central Europe. Mountainous, or *alpine*, Europe consists largely of the Alps, the stunning system of peaks that dominates the landscape of central and southern Europe. Unlike the more severe climates to the north, the climate of the lands surrounding the Mediterranean Sea is characterized by mild, rainy winters, and hot, dry summers.

Woodland

To the south of the northern polar regions lies a thick belt of *coniferous* forests. These forests are largely made up of evergreens—pine, spruce, and fir trees. The forests circle around the world and appear in northern Europe. South of these forests are *deciduous* forests, made up of trees such as oak, birch, and maple. Deciduous trees shed their leaves each fall.

Alpine

The Alps of Europe are a complex system of scenic peaks. Beginning in southeastern France, these rugged mountains run eastward across Switzerland, northern Italy, southern Germany, and Austria, and into Czechoslovakia. Other mountainous regions of Europe include the Pyrenees, which form the border between France and Spain. The Carpathian Mountains of eastern Europe form another major European mountain range.

Mediterranean

The coastline of the Mediterranean Sea follows a crooked course beginning at Spain. The coastline runs eastward and forms a boundary for such European nations as France, Italy, Yugoslavia, Albania, and Greece. Important Mediterranean islands include Corsica, Sardinia, and Sicily. The Mediterranean region is known for its year-round mild climate, beautiful beaches, and seaside scenery.

Norwegian Sea

Barents Sea

URAL MOUNTAINS

SWEDEN

FINLAND

NORWAY

Lake Onega

Lake Ladoga

Oslo

Helsinki

Leningrad

Lake Vanern

Stockholm

60°E

Lake Vattern

Volga River

DENMARK

Moscow

North Sea

Copenhagen

Baltic Sea

S O V I E T   U N I O N

ETH. Hamburg

NORTH EUROPEAN PLAIN

Amsterdam

Berlin

POLAND

Ural River

Bonn

EAST GERMANY

Warsaw

CENTRAL RUSSIAN UPLAND

LUX.

Kiev

Don River

Volgograd

WEST GERMANY

CZECHOSLOVAKIA

Rhine River

CARPATHIAN MOUNTAINS

Volga River

Munich

Vienna

SWITZ.

LIECH.

Danube River

AUSTRIA

Budapest

ALPS

HUNGARY

Mt. Blanc

ROMANIA

Milan

Caspian Sea

ITALY

YUGOSLAVIA

CAUCASUS MTS.

SAN MARINO

Adriatic Sea

CORSICA

APENNINES

Danube River

Black Sea

Rome

BULGARIA

ALBANIA

Istanbul

SARDINIA

GREECE

T U R K E Y

ranean Sea

SICILY

Athens

MALTA

CRETE

0	300	600 Mi.
0	300	600 Km.

Scale

30°E

©1990 Rand McNally & Co.

Woodland

Able to exist in populated areas, hedgehogs are common in Europe. Their bodies are covered with thick spines, and when threatened, they curl up into a ball. This posture is their main defense against attackers.

The coniferous, or evergreen, forests of northern Europe cover far more land than the deciduous forests to the south. These northern forests are the only European woodlands that have remained largely unchanged by human hands. The climate here is severe, with long, cold, snowy winters and short, cool summers. Nighttime hunters such as the red fox, hedgehog, and tawny owl prey upon a variety of insects, birds, and small rodents. During the day, such *herbivores* as rabbits and red deer peacefully munch plants. The pine marten, a member of the weasel family, remains common in these woodlands.

South of the evergreens lie forests of oak, ash, beech, and chestnut trees. The climate here is far less severe, and autumn brings the bright hues only these trees can offer. The limbs of these *broadleafed* trees are alive with birds, especially woodpeckers, jays, warblers, owls, and nightingales. On the shady forest floor, ornery boars and badgers search for food by rooting in the dirt.

Europe has long been settled, and today the continent is densely populated. The animals of Europe, especially those of the deciduous forests, have suffered from the loss of their habitat to human development.

The European bison, or wisent, became extinct in the wild in 1919. It was reintroduced in a protected area of Poland, where today it lives in the wild. Females, such as the one shown here, are smaller than males.

Unlike the horns of other animals, deer antlers are shed and grown again each year. Only males grow antlers, and they use them to fight over females. Shown here is a red deer, a species found in Europe.

Hares and rabbits are similar to each other. Hares are better runners, but rabbits are better at burrowing. Shown here is a European hare. Polecats are closely related to weasels. Wild boars, relatives of domestic pigs, are widely distributed in Europe, North Africa, and Asia. Squirrels are found worldwide; shown here is a red squirrel, common in Europe.

Alpine

Jagged peaks separated by deep, U-shaped valleys are typical of the alpine landscape. Evergreen forests at the lower elevations make the air smell of pine. Because the conditions of these fragrant woodlands are similar to those of the northern woodlands, some species, such as the capercaillie, are found in both regions.

Above the *treeline* lie the alpine meadows, home to such creatures as the ibex—a type of wild goat—and the marmot—a squirrel-like rodent. In spring, the meadows flower with color as wild plants like the *edelweiss* show off their blooms. Spring also brings migration, as both wild and domestic animals move to higher elevations with the warmer weather. The pattern reverses in fall. Above the meadows, life becomes more sparse as the landscape becomes barren rock and snow.

The wild animals of alpine Europe compete with humans and domestic animals for living space. Humans also cause pollution. Even the damming of rivers can cause problems for animals. In the Pyrenees, for example, a small rodent called the desman has become *vulnerable* because the streams in which it lives have been affected by dams.

The ibex is closely related to the chamois and to the mouflon. All three hoofed mammals live in European highlands. The ibex was saved from extinction, and now many of these animals graze the alpine meadows.

Mountain peaks provide a safe shelter for the lynx. It has been hunted to extinction in other parts of Europe. These cats are hunted because they sometimes prey on livestock. They are also killed for their luxurious fur.

Ground-dwelling birds called capercaillies are sometimes the victims of large birds of prey. The Pyrenees are home to the griffon vulture, a large, carnivorous bird. The majestic golden eagle, also a carnivore, is more widespread, as it is found in most of Europe and Asia. The chamois can scale steep mountainsides and thereby escape from predators.

Mediterranean

Summers near the blue waters of the Mediterranean Sea are almost desert-like. The brilliant sun blazes in a sky that is nearly always cloudless. Almost no rain falls, and many streams dry up. In winter, which is the rainy season, there are still many days of clear blue skies and balmy temperatures.

The Mediterranean region is a stopover place for many types of migrating birds. These birds live in Europe in the summer and in Africa in the winter. Here they rest before or after the long flight over the Sahara Desert of Africa and the Mediterranean Sea. Sea birds such as the oystercatcher and spoonbill are permanent residents.

The sandy dunes of the Mediterranean region support little plantlife. Because of a lack of food, few large animals live here. Farther inland, the vegetation becomes bushy, and such plant eaters as rabbits, hares, and fallow deer are found.

This region of the world has been inhabited by humans for centuries. Years and years of intensive settlement, agriculture, and forest clearance have taken their toll on the wildlife. Pollution in the Mediterranean Sea is also a threat to animals.

The Barbary macaque is a *vulnerable* species. It originated in the Atlas Mountains of North Africa but was introduced by humans to the craggy cliffs of Gibraltar. Today only thirty or forty of these handsome monkeys survive at Gibraltar.

The smallest of wild sheep, the mouflon inhabits southern Europe and some islands in the Mediterranean. The mouflon whistles and hisses when it is frightened. Relatives are the ibex and the American bighorn sheep.

Monk seals, such as the endangered Mediterranean monk seal, live in warm waters. Loggerhead turtles are a vulnerable species. They are found in *temperate* seas such as the Mediterranean. White storks do not nest in this region, but they are a regular sight. They migrate between Africa and Europe each year, crossing at Gibraltar and Turkey to avoid flying over long stretches of open water.

Asia

South of the Arctic Circle, northern Asia is a land of vast coniferous forests, or *taiga*. Below the taiga lies first a frigid grassland called *steppe* and then cold, windswept deserts. The Far East includes the most easterly Asian lands. Tibet, the highest plateau in the world, merges at its southwestern edge with the highest mountains in the world: the Himalayas. To the east is Szechwan, a part of China. India is a triangle of land in southern Asia. The warm, wet lands of Southeast Asia lie where mainland Asia breaks into thousands of islands.

Northern Asia

Just south of the northern Asian *tundra* lie the forests of Siberia, part of the Soviet Union. Below the forests, the Asian steppe reaches out from Europe and extends across the Soviet Union to the Far East. The Asian deserts begin at the Caspian Sea and the Plateau of Iran. They take in arid regions of the Soviet Union, China, and Mongolia, and end with the stony Gobi Desert.

The Far East

The Far East includes eastern China, the peninsula on which North and South Korea lie, and the islands of Japan. This is a forested land. The deciduous woodlands of the Far East are the only such forests found in northern Asia east of the Ural Mountains. This is also a mountainous land. There is little level ground on any of Japan's islands, and earthquakes and volcanoes are common.

The Himalayas, Tibet, and Szechwan

The Himalayas curve through northern Pakistan and India, almost all of Nepal and Bhutan, and southwestern China. The Plateau of Tibet is part of China. These are remote, high-altitude places with towering mountain spires and barren, windswept regions. In the Chinese region of Szechwan, the high elevations descend into gentle slopes with a mild climate and thick, lush forests.

India

Millions of years ago, India was not yet part of Asia. It was an island, moving slowly northward in the ancient seas. Finally, it crashed into the mainland, the impact forcing up the huge mountains that are today known as the Himalayas. The barren deserts of northwestern India contrast with the rest of the peninsula. It is warm and subject to monsoons, or periods of heavy rains.

Southeast Asia

The Southeast Asian nations of Malaysia, Indonesia, and the Philippines consist of thousands of islands. Some of them are tiny, and some are huge. The Malaysian and

90°E SIBERIA 120°E Amur River

SOVIET MANCHURIA

U N I O N Lake Baikal

M O N G O L I A Shenyang NORTH KOREA Sea of Japan Tokyo

Beijing Sŏul SOUTH KOREA JAPAN

GOBI (DESERT) Huang Yellow Sea East

TIEN SHAN River China

TARIM BASIN C H I N A Nanjing Shanghai Sea

Xi'an

PLATEAU Wuhan Tropic of Cancer

OF TIBET Chengdu T'aipei

SZECHWAN BASIN Chongqing Pacific

River Chang TAIWAN Ocean

Lhasa River

Brahmaputra Guangzhou

Delhi HIMALAYAS HONG KONG

NEPAL Mount BHUTAN

Ganges Everest Manila

River BANGLADESH Irrawaddy PHILIPPINES

I N D I A Calcutta BURMA Mekong South

V I E T N A M China

DECCAN L A O S Sea

River

(PLATEAU) THAILAND

Bangkok CAMBODIA

Bay of Bengal BRUNEI

ANDAMAN MALAYSIA

SRI ISLANDS BORNEO

LANKA MALAYSIA CELEBES

Equator

SINGAPORE

n Ocean I N D O N E S I A

SUMATRA

Jakarta JAVA

300 600 Mi.

300 600 Km.

Scale

Indonesian islands of Borneo and Sumatra
are among the largest in the world. This entire region lies within the tropics and is
warm year-round. Like India, Southeast
Asia experiences a summer monsoon
season.

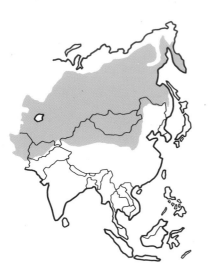

Northern Asia

The taiga of Asia is a wilderness of dark needleleaf evergreens. The landscape includes bogs, lakes, rivers, and streams. To the south, the steppe is a sea of grass that is cut by mighty rivers. It bursts with flowers in spring. The deserts are severe, stony plains under cloudless blue skies.

The vast Siberian forests are home to abundant wildlife. The brown bear and the elk are the most widespread. Predators here include sables, wolverines, lynxes, and owls. Their prey includes such rodents as squirrels, chipmunks, and voles.

On both the steppe and the desert, many varieties of rodents are found. Hamsters burrow below the plains, making systems of tunnels. Threats to the rodents are such predators as polecats, wolves, snakes, and eagles. A number of ground-nesting birds live here. Because of the absence of trees, they have learned to nest on the ground.

The hoofed mammals of north-central Asia include Bactrian camels, wild asses, wild horses, and saigas. The great herds of the animals are long gone, however. Hunting and competition with domestic animals for food and water have diminished their numbers.

The Asian wild ass lives in the driest regions of central Asia. Przewalski's horse is probably extinct in the wild but survives in zoos. It is the last remaining species of true wild horse. It has changed little since prehistoric times. This horse is believed to be the ancestor of the domestic horse. There are many species of gerbils. The one that is a popular pet is the Mongolian gerbil.

The two-humped Bactrian camel has mostly been tamed, but some wild ones are still found in the Gobi Desert. Camels are well suited to life in the desert, since they can survive long periods without water.

Wolves live in many habitats around the world but, in some places, have been wiped out by humans. The taiga of Siberia is one of the few places where many wolves are still found. Shown here is a gray, or timber, wolf.

The Far East

Summers in the Far East bring monsoons—the heavy, violent rains that soak both humans and beasts. Winters bring cold Arctic winds that blow down through the frozen lands to the north. The landscape here is forested, shifting from needleleaf conifers in the north to broadleaf, deciduous trees in the south.

According to fossil remains, the greatest of cats, the tiger, probably originated in this part of the world. Tigers later spread to other parts of Asia. Today, the Far East is the home of the Siberian tiger, the largest living *feline*. There are only about two hundred Siberian tigers still living in the wild. Tigers feed on wild boars, elk, and deer, which also inhabit the Far East. Smaller mammals here include squirrels and badgers.

The Manchurian or Japanese crane, a large bird that lives in Far Eastern marshes, is a vulnerable species. It has suffered from destruction of its habitat, part of which was destroyed during the Korean War (1950–1953). Other animals of the Far East suffer from loss of their habitats, as the forests of these heavily populated nations are cut down.

Asian black bears are also called moon bears, after a white, crescent-shaped patch of fur that grows on their chests. These bears live in brushy, forested areas of Asia, from Iran all the way to the Far East.

Swallowtail butterflies are found almost everywhere in the world, with several types living in the Far East. They are named for the shape of their wings, which resemble the tail of the swallow, a common bird. The raccoon dog is the only member of the dog family that does not bark. The wild boar has a large *range*—it is found in woodlands and steppes from Europe to Japan.

An endangered species, the sika deer inhabits forests of the Far East. These animals belong to a family of hoofed mammals that are found throughout the world. Like other members of the family, sika deer are herbivores.

The thick, warm fur of the Japanese macaque helps it survive the snowy winters of northern Japan. Macaques belong to a family of monkeys found all over Asia. Macaques are *omnivorous*, eating both plants and other animals.

The Himalayas, Tibet, and Szechwan

Here in the Himalayas and Tibet, often called the roof of the world, lives a remarkable variety of wildlife. Small furry mammals—such as pikas, voles, and marmots—scurry to find a meal in the rocky highlands. Farther down the slopes are the larger hoofed and horned animals, such as the markhor and tahr. These sure-footed animals are at home on the steep, rocky mountainsides. However, they sometimes fall prey to the skillful hunter of the slopes—the snow leopard.

Szechwan is a land of bamboo and rhododendron forests, where the sky is nearly always cloudy. Here among the bamboo trees live two species of panda. The giant panda may be one of the most well-known animals, but it is, in fact, one of the rarest on earth. Fewer than one thousand giant pandas exist in the wild, and they are rarely seen. Colorful pheasants probably originated in this part of Asia. Dozens of species of these birds exist. Some of them have been introduced by humans into North America and Europe.

Deforestation, or the clearing of trees, has caused some animals in this part of the world to lose their homes. The large human population of Szechwan is a threat to some species.

The most common prey of the snow leopard is the Siberian ibex, a wild goat. However, the most threatening hunters to ibexes, and to the other hoofed animals of the Himalayas, are not leopards—they are humans.

Although the red, or lesser, panda is more common than its giant relative, it is less known. Red pandas are excellent climbers and live in the remote, high-altitude bamboo forests of western China.

The elusive snow leopard is one of the most endangered animals in the world. Yet, these cats are still killed, and their beautiful fur is used to make garments. Many experts fear the leopard is headed for extinction.

Silk moths, of Chinese origin, make silk. Today they are found only in captivity. The thick fur of the endangered yak keeps it warm on the snowy heights of the Plateau of Tibet. The rare giant panda, not discovered by humans until 1869, lives only in a small region of cool, damp bamboo forest in China. The monkey known as the Hanuman langur is common in this part of Asia.

India

Cobras such as this Indian cobra are characterized by a hood at the neck. These poisonous snakes rear up and spread their hood when they are frightened or excited. Like all other snakes, cobras are deaf.

Indian winters are cool and dry. The skies are cloudless, and the humidity is low. In March, the temperatures begin to rise, and the heat becomes unbearable. In June the monsoon season arrives. The air is thick with humidity, and it rains every day.

After India merged with the rest of Asia, animals from Africa and northern Asia found their way into the Indian peninsula. Some of the animals of the African and Middle Eastern deserts have migrated as far as arid northwestern India. The hyena and jackal, both doglike scavengers, are two such animals. Another animal that lives in both Africa and India is the mongoose. This small furry carnivore is found in abundance in many Indian locales. Closely related to mongooses are civets, which inhabit tropical forests all over southern Asia.

India has the second largest human population of all the nations in the world. As a result, people and animals compete for space. People, who need land for cities, houses, and farms, are winning the battle. Therefore, the habitats of many beautiful Indian animals are being destroyed. In regions too remote for humans, however, rare Indian animals can still be found.

Peafowl may still fly free in the thickest Indian forests. Water buffalo were once widespread but today are found in the wild only in remote regions. Tigers, the largest of all cats, are an endangered species. Only a few thousand survive in India. The Asian elephant is smaller, with far smaller ears, than its African counterpart. It, too, is endangered.

The gharial is a type of crocodile found in the rivers of India. It is distinguished by its narrow jaw and snout. Considered sacred by many Indians, the endangered gharial rarely attacks humans.

Southeast Asia

F ar away from the populated regions of Southeast Asia lies an untamed *terrain* that is difficult for people to reach. Mountains with sharp ridges and deep gorges make traveling difficult. Hot, dank forests with dense, tangled undergrowth make it even harder. Along the many miles of coastline, mangrove trees abound, their roots forming tangles in the swampy waters.

The Southeast Asian rain forests are home to a great variety of wildlife. In the treetops, unusual reptiles, frogs, and squirrels have developed webbed limbs that catch the air and let them glide from tree to tree. The colugo is a gliding mammal that is not clearly related to any other animal.

Langurs and macaques, two types of monkeys, are also suited to life in the trees. The vulnerable *proboscis* monkey, with its huge nose, inhabits the low rain forests of Borneo. Bats, which make up about one-quarter of all species of mammals, flit about in the night forest.

The nations of Southeast Asia are among the world's most densely populated, and the tropical forests here are disappearing at an alarming rate. Wild animals who live in the forests are becoming rarer.

The orang-utan is a large red ape that lives in trees. Its name means "man of the woods." Found only in the forests of Sumatra and Borneo, orang-utans are endangered, a result of hunting and habitat loss.

Mudskippers are fish that can breathe air. Thus, they spend about as much time out of water as in it. Several species of mudskippers live along warm, muddy shorelines of Southeast Asian mangrove swamps.

The huge eyes of the nocturnal tarsier help it to find prey in the dark. Tarsiers are primates, like apes and monkeys, and live only in Southeast Asia. The Philippine tarsier, shown here, is endangered.

The vulnerable clouded leopard is a skilled climber that can run down trees head first. Flying foxes are not foxes at all, but bats. The common flying fox is a very large bat that is found in several regions of the world, including Southeast Asia. Found in South America as well as Southeast Asia, tapirs may look like pigs or elephants but are in fact related to horses and rhinoceroses.

Africa and the Middle East

Much of northern and some of southern Africa is dry, rocky desert. The harsh desert habitat extends into the Middle East. South of the Sahara, curving around to the east, and reaching into the south are grasslands known as *savanna*. The equator runs through the middle of Africa. In western Africa, the low-lying lands along the equator and to the northwest of the equator receive much rainfall. This is where the African rain forests lie. Along the equator in East Africa, the terrain is higher, even mountainous, and less rain falls. Off Africa's southeastern coast lies Madagascar, the fourth largest island in the world.

Savanna

Between the African deserts and rain forests are huge regions of grassland. In the north, the African savanna lies in such regions as northern Nigeria and southern Chad. In East Africa, there are lakes and mountains, but there are well-known areas of savanna here as well. The grasslands curve to the south into Tanzania, then on to Zaire and Angola. Colors here vary according to season. In the dry season, usually July to October, the savanna is an ocean of browns. In the rainy season, generally December to May, the savanna becomes a sea of greens.

Rain Forest

Most of the tropical rain forests of Africa are found in and around the Congo Basin, an area drained by the Congo and Ubangi rivers. This region straddles the equator. Most of it lies in northern Zaire. It extends into other nations such as the Central African Republic, the Congo, and Gabon. The forests are also found along the coasts of such West African nations as Nigeria and Ghana.

Desert

The world's largest desert region begins in western Africa at the Atlantic coasts of Mauritania and Western Sahara. It extends across the Sahara of North Africa all the way to Egypt. The desert conditions continue east of the Red Sea into the Asian portion of the Middle East. In southern Africa, the Kalahari Desert covers a large portion of Botswana. The Namib Desert lies along the coast of Namibia.

East Africa

The tropical highlands of East Africa take in parts of several nations. Among them are Ethiopia, Uganda, Rwanda, Burundi, Zaire, Kenya, and Tanzania. Here the mountains reach great heights. As a result, the climate, vegetation, and wildlife vary from those of the surrounding lands. Between the mountains is the Rift Valley, parts of which have filled with water to form a series of beautiful lakes.

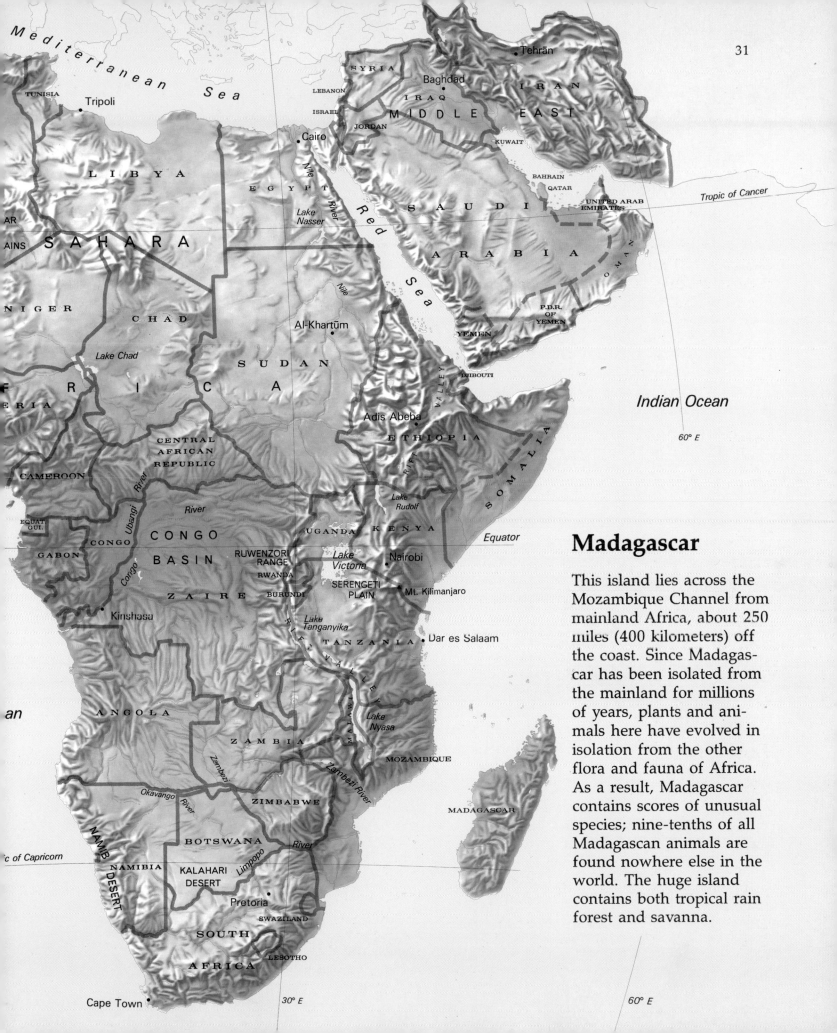

Mediterranean Sea

TUNISIA
Tripoli

LIBYA

SAHARA

AR
AINS

NIGER

CHAD

Lake Chad

FRICA

ERIA

CAMEROON

EQUAT.
GUI.

GABON

CONGO

CONGO
BASIN

ZAIRE

Ubangi River

River

Corrigo

Kinshasa

ANGOLA

ZAMBIA

Zambezi

Okavango River

ZIMBABWE

NAMIB DESERT

NAMIBIA

BOTSWANA

KALAHARI
DESERT

c of Capricorn

Limpopo River

Pretoria

SWAZILAND

SOUTH

AFRICA

LESOTHO

Cape Town

an

30° E

CENTRAL
AFRICAN
REPUBLIC

E
G
Y
P
T

Cairo

Lake
Nasser

Nile River

SUDAN

Al-Khartūm

Nile

RUWENZORI
RANGE

RWANDA

BURUNDI

Lake
Tanganyika

Lake
Victoria

SERENGETI
PLAIN

UGANDA

KENYA

Nairobi

Mt. Kilimanjaro

TANZANIA

Dar es Salaam

Lake
Nyasa

MALAWI

Zambezi River

MOZAMBIQUE

RIFT VALLEY

Adis Abeba

ETHIOPIA

Lake
Rudolf

SOMALIA

DJIBOUTI

RIFT VALLEY

Red Sea

SYRIA

LEBANON

ISRAEL

JORDAN

Baghdad

IRAQ

Tehrān

IRAN

MIDDLE EAST

KUWAIT

SAUDI

ARABIA

BAHRAIN

QATAR

UNITED ARAB
EMIRATES

OMAN

P.D.R.
OF
YEMEN

YEMEN

Tropic of Cancer

Indian Ocean

60° E

Equator

MADAGASCAR

60° E

Madagascar

This island lies across the Mozambique Channel from mainland Africa, about 250 miles (400 kilometers) off the coast. Since Madagascar has been isolated from the mainland for millions of years, plants and animals here have evolved in isolation from the other flora and fauna of Africa. As a result, Madagascar contains scores of unusual species; nine-tenths of all Madagascan animals are found nowhere else in the world. The huge island contains both tropical rain forest and savanna.

Savanna

Giraffes can grow taller than fifteen feet (about five meters), making them the tallest animals on the savanna. Their height allows them to browse the upper branches of trees, where other animals cannot reach.

The vast grasslands, or savanna, of Africa stretch out as far as the eye can see. In some places almost treeless, the savanna is a sun-drenched flatland that teems with wildlife. Here are found some of the most famous and spectacular animals in the world.

In protected areas, the swaying grasses are alive with herds of elephants, giraffes, zebras, antelopes, gazelles, wildebeests, and many other grazing mammals. These animals roam the savanna, migrating across huge distances in search of food and water. Each species has a particular set of habits that allows it to eat and live side-by-side with other species, without competing for food.

Predators such as lions, cheetahs, and wild dogs stalk these animals. These hunters hide in the grasses, waiting for the right moment for the chase. Predators are normally far fewer in number than the animals upon which they prey.

The animals of the savanna share a common enemy: humans. One threat is *poachers* who illegally kill animals for their hides, horns, or tusks. Another danger is fences erected by farmers to enclose their herds. These fences prevent migrating wild animals from moving freely in their seasonal searches for food and water.

The maneless female lioness does most of the hunting for a group, or *pride*, of lions. Often other carnivores on the savanna benefit from her hunt. Striped zebras are among the lioness's favorite prey. When the lions have finished feeding, doglike hyenas might move in and feed on the leftovers. Finally, vultures swoop down from the skies to finish off the carcass.

A few years ago, African elephants numbered 1.3 million. Today, there are fewer than half that number because they have been slaughtered for their ivory tusks. The African elephant recently became an endangered species.

Reaching speeds of sixty miles (ninety-six kilometers) per hour during a chase, cheetahs are the world's fastest land animals. Loss of habitat and the fur trade threaten these graceful cats, which are a vulnerable species.

Rain Forest

In the rain forest, the weather can be monotonous: every day is hot and wet, every week is hot and wet, and every month is hot and wet. Under the canopy of high trees, there is not much light. Vines and garlands hang from the trees, creating a gloomy, almost eerie world of heavy shade.

The open floor in the African rain forest is home to hoofed grazing mammals such as the okapi, chevrotain, duiker, and bongo. These animals are striped and spotted in ways that help camouflage them from predators. Such larger animals as elephants, leopards, and gorillas also make their homes here. In the treetops live colorful parrots, hornbills, and several types of monkeys. Rain forests are typically home to a huge variety of insects, which includes the much-feared driver, or army, ant. These insects march along in wide columns and devour anything that may lie in their path.

Like other rain forests, those of Africa are in danger. Logging and farming are two major threats. Population growth in countries along the equator has brought increased demand for land. As a result the forests are cleared. The animals are losing their habitat, and their numbers have been decreasing.

Mandrills live near the floor of the rain forest, along with gorillas and chimpanzees. Mandrills, a type of baboon, are the largest monkeys. They will eat almost anything they find in the rain forest.

The bush babies of the African rain forest are very similar to the lemurs of Madagascar. The large eyes of the nocturnal bush baby help it see at night. Its long hind legs help it leap from tree to tree.

The chimpanzee, a vulnerable species, is a very intelligent animal. The scales of the armored pangolin protect it from most predators. The okapi is a close relative of the giraffe. Leopards live in a wide variety of habitats, including African rain forests. Hunted for their beautiful spotted coats, leopards are also a vulnerable species.

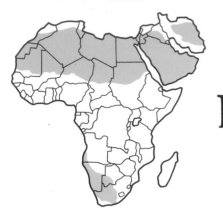

Desert

The meerkat, or suricate, is a type of mongoose that lives in the dry regions of southern Africa. Meerkats often strike poses such as the one above so they can see what is happening around the burrows in which they live.

I n the Sahara, the temperatures are the highest on earth. The amount of *precipitation* (rain, dew, or snow) is the lowest on earth. Here the environment is so hostile, and food and water so scanty, that life scarcely exists.

It is the never-ending struggle to find water that dominates the lives of many desert animals. Those animals that do survive have developed different ways of winning this struggle. The addax, for example, never drinks. It is a grazing antelope that gets all the water it needs from the plants it eats. The sandgrouse is a bird that flies far to find water. When it does, it soaks its feathers to take water back to its family. The camel or dromedary is the most famous animal of the desert. Camels can go for long periods of time without drinking water.

The harsh terrain and climate of the desert discourage habitation, not only by wildlife but also by humans. For many years, the animals that survived in the African deserts did so without fear of human interference. The discovery of oil in the deserts of North Africa changed all that. Today the search for oil creates danger for the animals and their desert habitat.

Monitor lizards live in a variety of habitats, including the Sahara. Scorpions also live in many places, but mostly in deserts. The sting of some scorpions can be fatal to humans. Once a wild animal, the one-humped dromedary is now a completely domesticated species. The tiny fennec fox roams northern Africa and parts of the Middle East.

The scimitar-horned oryx once roamed freely over North Africa. This graceful animal, along with its close relative the Arabian oryx, was hunted almost to extinction. Efforts are now being made to save the endangered oryx.

The high deserts of northern Africa are home to the Barbary sheep. This species belongs to a large family of goat antelopes, with relatives all over the world. Barbary sheep are a vulnerable species.

East Africa

The mountains of East Africa are tropical highland islands in a sea of lowland savanna grasslands. On the plains below lies the savanna with its array of wildlife. Some species, like the elephant and black rhinoceros, travel from the savanna into the forests at the mountains' lower altitudes in search of food. Leopards venture quite far up the mountains in their quest for prey.

Farther up the slopes, however, species that live only in the mountains are found. In the lush, shady forests, for example, lives the mountain gorilla, a *primate*. Several species of monkeys, birds, and hyraxes appear. Eagles and hawks haunt the craggy peaks. The tops of mountains are also known for bizarre plant life. This has gained the Ruwenzori Range the nickname ''Mountains of the Moon.''

The Rift Valley is a huge gash in the face of the earth. The lakes lying in the East African part of the valley are home to their own species of animals. Many types of fish and birds inhabit the waters. Among the birds are lily trotters, which scoot across the water by walking on lily pads. Among the fish are cichlids, which carry their eggs in their mouths.

High in the mountains of East Africa, only a few hundred highly endangered mountain gorillas survive. Deforestation, hunting, and capture for zoos threaten these magnificent primates with extinction.

Although hyraxes look like rodents, they are related to elephants and aardvarks. Several varieties of hyraxes are found in Africa. Tree hyraxes, such as the one shown here, are found in the mountain forests of East Africa.

Rhinoceroses are often seen with birds called oxpeckers. Their relationship benefits both the rhinos and the birds. Insects living on the rhinos are food for the oxpeckers, who rid the rhinos of these pests.

Crocodiles, hippopotamuses, and flamingos are found near African waters. By night the huge but gentle hippopotamus grazes the grasslands, but, like the crocodile, spends hot African days wallowing in water or mud. The fearsome-looking crocodile is more threatened than threatening, as it is poached for its skin. Graceful flamingos are found in abundance in East African lakes.

Madagascar

Some people have said that visiting Madagascar is like visiting another world because the plants and animals here are unique. The first people to arrive on Madagascar found a fabulous variety of creatures—including huge flightless birds, giant tortoises, and giant lemurs. They did not find many other types of animals, however. One of the remarkable things about Madagascan wildlife is its lack of some common types of animals.

Today, Madagascar is the home of lemurs, chameleons, and tenrecs. It is also home of the fist-sized lesser mouselemur, the smallest primate in the world. There are no rabbits on Madagascar, but the giant jumping rat looks and acts like one. Although the aye-aye is harmless, it is feared as a death omen by the people of Madagascar. It is killed on sight. Other Madagascan species include unusual tortoises and lizards.

Three-quarters of the world's species of chameleons live on Madagascar. Among other unusual capabilities, chameleons can change the color of their skin. The aye-aye is an endangered primate. Mongooses are widely distributed throughout Africa and Asia, and several species live on Madagascar. A variety of shrewlike mammals called tenrecs also live on Madagascar.

When humans arrived, much of the island was forested. Four-fifths of the Madagascan forest has been cut down, however, and the remaining forests are going fast. Lemurs and the other forest-dwelling animals are losing their habitat. Therefore, some experts consider most Madagascan animals endangered.

Like monkeys and apes, lemurs are primates. Having evolved in isolation from other animals, lemurs live only on Madagascar and on nearby islands. Shown here are ring-tailed lemurs, one of many species found on Madagascar.

This is a ruffed lemur, one of the largest lemur species. Ruffed lemurs are about as big as large house cats. Like most lemurs, ruffed lemurs spend most of their time high in the trees of Madagascar.

Oceania

In the south and central Pacific Ocean lie thousands of islands. Australia is an island, but it is so big, it is considered a continent. The next largest island here is New Guinea. Along with many of the small islands that lie within the tropics, New Guinea has a warm, wet climate. So does much of Australia's Cape York Peninsula. But this is one of the few parts of Australia that has a wet climate. Most of Australia is arid, receiving very little precipitation. Off Australia's southeast coast is the island of Tasmania. Farther away, across the Tasman Sea, is New Zealand.

Tropical Australia and New Guinea

The huge island of New Guinea is the second largest island in the world, after Greenland. A narrow strip of water called Torres Strait separates the island of New Guinea from Australia's Cape York Peninsula. This extreme northern region of Australia and New Guinea are mostly covered with tropical rain forests. At one time, millions of years ago, geologists theorize that these regions were joined. There are more tropical forests in the northern part of Arnhem Land and along the northeastern coast of Australia, east of the Great Dividing Range.

Arid Australia

Except for Antarctica, Australia is the driest continent. More than two-thirds of Australia is desertlike. In fact, Australia's dry interior contains the largest desert region in the Southern Hemisphere. Australians call this region the Outback. Two of the major deserts here are the Great Sandy Desert and the Great Victoria Desert. Like other desert regions, seasons have little meaning here. The sun almost always shines, and the days are always hot. Arid Australia is not without plant life. Outside of the deserts, the Outback of Australia is scrubby grassland.

120°W

INDONE

Darwin

Indian

Ocean

GREAT SANDY DESERT

MACD
RAN
Alice S

GIBSON DESERT

A U S T

GREAT VICTORIA
DESERT

Perth

Great Australi
Bight

Southeastern Australia, Tasmania, and New Zealand

The southeastern corner of Australia experiences the most moderate climate on the continent. Here rainfall is plentiful. Though there are four distinct seasons, temperatures are never really hot nor really cold. Across the Bass Strait lies Tasmania, which experiences a cooler and wetter climate than southeastern Australia. Tasmania, which is part of the nation of Australia, is covered with mountains and hills, with small valleys between them. To the east are two islands called North Island and South Island. Together with several smaller islands, they form the boot-shaped nation of New Zealand. This is a rugged, windswept land, with green slopes of snow-capped mountains plunging nearly into the sea.

Equator

150°W

PAPUA NEW GUINEA

NEW GUINEA

afura Sea

Torres Strait

Port Moresby

SOLOMON ISLANDS

CAPE YORK PENINSULA

Gulf of Carpentaria

GREAT BARRIER REEF

VANUATU

NEW HEBRIDES

Coral Sea

FIJI

NEW CALEDONIA

GREAT DIVIDING RANGE

A L I A

Lake Eyre

Brisbane

TONGA

Tropic of Capricorn

Darling River

Murray River

Adelaide

Canberra

Sydney

Pacific Ocean

Melbourne

Bass Strait

Tasman Sea

TASMANIA

NEW ZEALAND

NORTH ISLAND

Hobart

Wellington

SOUTH ISLAND

0   300   600 Mi.

0   300   600 Km.

Scale

180°

Tropical Australia and New Guinea

New Guinea is an exotic land of dripping rain forests, snow-tipped mountains, and abundant wildlife. And, tucked away in remote pockets, are primitive human cultures. Nearby, the forests of northeastern Australia possess many of the same characteristics and animals.

The bird life found here is particularly spectacular, especially birds of paradise. There are more than forty species of these birds, each with its own type of brilliant feathers. As is common among birds, only the males have such showy plumage, which they display to attract the far more drab females. Other birds include cockatoos, parrots, and cassowaries—giant flightless birds that are capable of killing with one kick of their powerful legs.

Such *marsupials* as possums, cuscuses, and gliders inhabit the trees of the dense forests. Gliders' small size and skin flaps between their limbs enable them to stretch out and catch the air when they leap from tree to tree.

Much of the forest of New Guinea and northern Australia has been lost to timber production. As a result, many species of animals are losing their habitats and are quickly becoming extinct.

Pigeons are common throughout the world. There are more than forty species of pigeons on the island of New Guinea. The Victoria crowned pigeon inhabits the forests of the northern part of the island.

Related to the platypus, the echidna is found throughout Australia and New Guinea. Like platypuses, echidnas are mammals that lay eggs. Ants and termites are the preferred foods of this short-beaked echidna.

Dugongs inhabit the shallow waters of this region. As a result of overhunting, dugongs have become a vulnerable species. The cuscus is a marsupial. Several species of cuscuses are found on New Guinea, Australia, and neighboring islands. Birds of paradise possess magnificent plumage. Several species have been hunted to the verge of extinction because of demand for their feathers.

Arid Australia

Central Australia is a land of deserts. Here lie sandy deserts and rocky deserts, mountainous deserts and flat clay deserts. A dominant color is red. Ayers Rock, near Alice Springs, is a huge and ancient piece of red sandstone that rises steeply from the barren scrubland that surrounds it.

Although the vast interior of Australia is desert or nearly so, it is not lifeless. On the contrary, the grasslands here boast many unique species of wild animals. Of special interest in Australia are the many varieties of warm-blooded mammals called *marsupials*. Most marsupials bear undeveloped young, which make their way to their mother's pouch, where they spend more time growing. In arid Australia, several marsupial varieties are found. Kangaroos are the most well known, but other marsupials, such as wombats and bandicoots, are found here as well.

A number of Australian marsupials are threatened. Wombats and bandicoots must compete with domestic animals for the sparse food of the environments in which they live. Several types of wallabies, small members of the kangaroo family, have become extinct, principally because of overhunting.

This hairy-nosed wombat is closely related to the koala. Unlike koalas, however, wombats live on the ground, in extensive burrows or warrens. Like other marsupials, wombats have pouches in which they raise their young.

When threatened, the frilled lizard opens wide its mouth, extends a cape of skin around its neck, and sways back and forth. If further provoked, the lizard approaches the intruder, emitting a low hiss.

Emus are Australia's largest birds. They
have been hunted because they graze on
grasses and thereby compete with domestic animals for food. Emus' wings are
quite small, and they do not fly.

It is believed that wild dogs called *dingoes* are descended from tame dogs brought
to Australia by humans thousands of years ago. Ratlike bandicoots are marsupials,
and they are found all over Australia. All members of the cockatoo family have
crests. The smallest member is the cockatiel, shown here. The best-known parakeet is the budgerigar of central and southern Australia.

Southeastern Australia, Tasmania, & New Zealand

B etween the coast of southeastern Australia and the summits of the Great Dividing Range are forests of *eucalyptus* trees. Some types are mere bushes, while others grow up to three hundred feet (ninety meters) high. And, some species are the food of the koala, the bearlike marsupial found only in these forests.

On Tasmania resides the platypus and such marsupials as wombats, gliders, and wallabies. Here also are three types of marsupial predators: the Tasmanian wolf, the Tasmanian devil, and the tiger cat. The Tasmanian wolf is not a wolf at all, but a rela- tively large, doglike animal that might be extinct.

New Zealand is a remote land, and few land animals have migrated here from other places. The tuatara is one of the remaining relics from the days when dinosaurs roamed the earth. Because of the absence of predators, flightless birds have been able to live on New Zealand. The rare kakapo is a ground-dwelling member of the parrot family. The kiwi is another flightless bird. With the introduction of such domestic predators as dogs and cats, the number of these birds has declined. Today they are threatened.

Tasmanian devils are the largest of Australia's marsupial carnivores. They can kill larger animals such as sheep. Once widely distributed, the Tasmanian devil is now found only on Tasmania.

Tuataras inhabit islands off New Zealand. They are rare animals and are the only remaining species of an otherwise extinct family of reptiles. Tuataras live in burrows, which they share with birds called *petrels*.

Along with macaws, budgerigars, and cockatoos, lorikeets are members of the parrot family. Like other parrots, the rainbow lorikeets shown here are threatened by habitat destruction and by the pet trade.

Platypuses are egg-laying mammals that spend much of their time looking for food in the streams and lakes beside which they make their burrows. Koalas, which are marsupials, live in eucalyptus forests. Unfortunately, the forests are being cut down. Many species of kangaroos, also marsupials, are found in Australia. Shown here is one of the biggest species, the gray kangaroo.

North America

The western part of North America is largely mountainous. Chief among the many ranges here are the Rocky Mountains, which extend from northwestern Canada to the southwestern United States. The Great Plains are the flatlands east of the mountains that contain vast North American grasslands and croplands. To the east lie forested areas and, in the southeastern United States, huge swamps. To the south is the narrow strip of land that connects North and South America. It is a wet, warm region called Central America. Central America has a tropical climate, which is similar to that of the islands in the Caribbean Sea.

Western Mountains

Beginning in Alaska, the great northern *cordillera*, or mountain system, runs southward through the western Canadian provinces and the western United States. In addition to the Rocky Mountains, major ranges include the Brooks and Alaska ranges, the Mackenzie and Coast mountains, the Cascade and Coast ranges, and the Sierra Nevada. Many of these mountains are younger than eastern ranges such as the Appalachians. They have not been exposed to the wind and weather as long. As a result, they are rougher and more rugged than the more eroded ranges to the east.

Great Plains

Central North America was once covered by a huge inland sea. When the waters retreated, a flatland emerged, and the Great Plains took shape. Today, the Great Plains extend from the edge of the deciduous forests in the east to the Rocky Mountains in the west, and from the Saskatchewan River in the north southward to the Gulf of Mexico. There is little that obstructs the line of the horizon in the Great Plains. The plains are a flat or gently rolling land, with very few trees, and they stretch out in every direction for miles and miles. The sky seems huge here, and it frequently flashes and crashes with violent thunderstorms.

Eastern Forests and Swamps

Reaching down into the Great Lakes area and the states of the Northeast are the coniferous, or pine, forests of northeastern North America. They give

way to broadleaf, deciduous forests. These extend from the Great Lakes across the Appalachians to the southern coastal plains. Lowland forests and swamps exist in the southeastern United States. Most well-known among the swamplands is the Everglades of Florida.

Central America and Caribbean

The tropical region known as Central America forms a land bridge between two great continents. It is a mountainous region—the place where the western mountains of North America merge with the Andes of South America. It is also a land of earthquakes and active volcanoes. Many Caribbean islands are mountainous, too. Some of them were formed by huge volcanoes that reach up from the ocean floor.

©1990 Rand McNally & Co.

Western Mountains

The Coast Ranges rise from the rocky Pacific coast. Their slopes are lush with fir and spruce trees, forming shadowy cover for the ferns below. The Cascades are snow-covered volcanic cones. The mighty Rockies tower thousands of feet, thrusting jagged peaks and sawtooth ridges high into the cold, thin air. This is the home of some of North America's most spectacular wildlife.

In the northern mountains lives the grizzly bear. This huge predator loves to feed on the salmon it catches in icy, clear northern streams. Some streams may be dammed, not by humans, but by the beaver, which fells trees for the dam with its big, sharp teeth.

The lynx and the puma are the *feline* predators of the mountains. Among their prey are bighorn sheep, mule deer, and mountain goats—three of the hoofed, grazing animals of the region. Smaller mammals include hoary marmots, minks, porcupines, squirrels, chipmunks, and opossums.

Many protected areas in the western mountains provide the animals with lots of wilderness. Yet, the demands of the industrialized nations of the United States and Canada take their toll on the habitat as forests are cut and pollution spreads.

The North American porcupine inhabits forested regions in much of the continent. Porcupines do not see well. They rely on their quills and on their keen senses of hearing and smell to protect them from predators.

The national bird of the United States is the bald eagle. Pesticides are a problem for eagles, because these poisons get into their food. The eagles' eggs are affected, and they do not hatch well. As the result, these birds are threatened.

Mountain goats are found mainly in peaks of the Northwest. These animals prefer living on steep cliffs in places where there is plenty of snow. The horns of the mountain goat are small but very sharp.

Cougars—also called pumas, mountain lions, or panthers—are the largest of all wild North American cats. Grizzly, or brown, bears were once more common, but hunting and loss of habitat have diminished their numbers. The elk is in the deer family, and it loses and regrows its antlers every year. The American bighorn sheep is related to the mountain goat, and its horns are permanent.

Great Plains

The Great Plains are sometimes gently rolling and sometimes flat as a table. Except where crops are grown, they are always grassy and always stretching out in every direction. On the western edge, yearly rainfall is slight, and the grasses are short and scrubby. The central plains receive more rainfall, and the grass grows taller. At the eastern edge, where rainfall is plentiful, the swaying grasses can grow taller than people.

Other large mammals have disappeared with the advance of civilization across the grasslands, but not the coyote. In fact, the coyote has been able to increase its range as competition for food has decreased. Coyotes prey on prairie dogs, mice, jackrabbits, and sometimes on domestic animals. Birds of the Great Plains include prairie falcons and prairie chickens. The song of the meadowlark, along with the howl of the coyote, is often associated with the Great Plains.

The wild grasslands of the Great Plains have been turned into what may be the world's most productive agricultural region. Today very little original prairie exists. The animals here have been forced from their homes, and many of them have been hunted to near extinction.

The fur trade poses a serious threat to most wild cats, including the bobcat. Probably named for its short tail, the bobcat is found in a variety of habitats, including the plains between southern Canada and northern Mexico.

Coyotes are a familiar symbol of the American West. In 1850, fifty million pronghorns roamed the prairie. By 1920, hunters had reduced that number to about thirteen thousand. The American bison suffered a similar fate and nearly became extinct. Conservation efforts were made to save both species. Today large numbers of them are found in protected areas on the Great Plains.

Rattlesnakes, named for the rattles on their tails, are venomous snakes that squirt poison through their fangs into their victims. Rattlesnakes are found in many parts of North America, including the Great Plains.

A close relative of the squirrel, the black-tailed prairie dog lives in burrows on the Great Plains. These burrows are interconnected, forming prairie-dog towns that may take up many acres.

Eastern Forests and Swamps

In summer, the trees form a lush green tangle that shades the cool forest floor. Fall is a splash of color, as the leaves turn yellow, gold, red, and brown, and then fall from the trees. In winter, the thin rays of the sun fall through the bare branches but do little to warm the silent, snow-clad forest. Spring brings another colorful display as wildflowers make their brief appearance. Such are the four seasons in the eastern forests of North America.

At one time, a squirrel hopping through the highest tree branches could go from Pennsylvania to Alabama without touching the ground. Today, however, much of the eastern forest has been cut down, and some species, such as wolves and mountain lions, have disappeared. Foxes, weasels, and skunks are now the main hunters. They feed on such smaller animals as squirrels, chipmunks, and mice.

As the squirrel headed southeast, it would find the land getting lower and swamps and marshes more common. The types of trees would change, too, and at the tip of Florida, it would find itself in the mangroves and cypresses of the Everglades. These swamps are being drained to make farmland. Also, they are polluted by the heavily populated regions that surround them.

Once a threatened species, white-tailed deer now abound in eastern forests. As male deer mature, their antlers appear with more branches, or points. White-tailed deer are born with white spots, which fade as they mature.

In the remaining forests of North America, the black bear is not an uncommon sight. Black bears are smaller than brown bears. Like most bears, black bears are omnivorous, eating just about anything they can find.

Bullfrogs live in the ponds and marshes of eastern North America. Bullfrogs wait in the water for their prey, usually insects. At the right moment, the frogs leap with their powerful back legs to catch their meal.

Cottontail rabbits thrive in heavily populated areas such as those of eastern North America. So do raccoons, which resemble masked bandits. Alligators and great white herons are residents of southeastern North American swamps. Alligators were hunted for their skins until they were in danger of extinction. Since coming under protection, their number has increased.

Central America and the Caribbean

High in the mountains of Central America are regions known as cloud forests—where clouds sweep over the lush green vegetation. Alpine meadows are found here as well. Below lie forests and swamps.

In the forests, small wild cats such as the margay cat and the ocelot prowl in the night. They take such prey as monkeys, opossums, and iguanas. The forests are far from silent, as they are home to a great concentration of birds. Some of them spend winters here and return to North America in the spring. Howler, spider, and woolly monkeys hang from the branches with the aid of their *prehensile* tails, which are capable of wrapping and gripping.

The islands of the Caribbean are isolated from the mainland. Large wild animals have never found their way out to them. Birds are the main form of wildlife here, and many of the islands boast their own species of parrot. Habitat destruction and hunting threaten the parrots of the Caribbean, and many of them are endangered. Sadly, these birds are not the only animals in danger in this region, as deforestation and hunting take their toll in Central America.

The bright-red plumage of the scarlet ibis is acquired as the bird matures. The red becomes more intense as the bird gets older. These birds inhabit swamplands, and their long bills are used to probe the mud for food.

The iguana family consists of many different lizards, including the green iguana shown here. Green iguanas inhabit the tropical forests of Central America and some Caribbean islands.

The most serious threat to margay cats is the fur trade. Thousands of these beautifully spotted cats are killed each year, and they are now a vulnerable species. Margay cats are found throughout Central America.

Little is known about the elusive kinkajou. The quetzal, a stunning Central American bird, is known for its long, bright green tail plumage. Tapirs found in Central America are similar to those found in Southeast Asia. The long snouts of anteaters help them locate their favorite foods—ants and termites. The bony plates of the armadillo protect it from attackers.

South America

The Amazon River cuts across northern South America, forming the largest river system in the world along the way. In the basin of the Amazon River and along some coasts of Brazil are the great rain forests of South America. South of the Amazon region lies the Gran Chaco, a dry region with few trees, and the Pampa, a grassland that receives more rain than the Gran Chaco. The peaks of the Andes form the world's longest chain of mountains. They run down the entire western side of South America. In the Pacific Ocean, off the west coast of South America, lie the Galápagos Islands.

Rain Forest

The hot, wet lands along the Amazon River, near the equator, form the largest rain forest in the world. The forest comprises large chunks of Brazil, Peru, Ecuador, and Colombia. Rain forests are also found along the coast of Brazil, near Rio de Janeiro. Rain forests are characterized by a large number of animal species, especially insects and marine-dwelling creatures. It is estimated that nearly one-quarter of all species alive in the world today live in South America.

Gran Chaco and Pampa

The dry lands of the Gran Chaco lie in southern Bolivia, Argentina, and Paraguay. Here the arid plains stretch out, dotted with clumps of trees. The Pampa is farther south in Argentina and Uruguay. It reaches down into the steppe of Patagonia. The Gran Chaco and Pampa are the great grasslands of South America. They are, roughly, the South American counterpart to the African savanna.

Andes

The rugged Andes are found in every nation in western South America: Colombia, Ecuador, Peru, Bolivia, Chile, and Argentina. After the Himalayas of Asia, the Andes are the second highest mountain range in the world, and they are the world's longest continuous chain of mountains. They are young mountains, and frequent earthquakes and volcanoes here are evidence that the Andes are still rising.

Caribbean Sea

90°W

60°W

ANDES

Lake
Maracaibo

• Caracas

Orinoco River

VENEZUELA

Angel Falls

GUYANA

FRENCH GUIANA

LLANOS

GUIANA HIGHLANDS

SURINAME

• Bogotá

COLOMBIA

Equator

GALÁPAGOS
ISLANDS

Quito •

ECUADOR

Negro R.

• Belém

Manaus •

Amazon River

Tapajós River

Pacific
Ocean

ANDES

S E L V A S

Fortaleza •

PERU

B   R   A   Z   I   L

• Lima

B R A Z I L I A N

Lake Titicaca

H I G H L A N D S

BOLIVIA

M A T O
G R O S S O
P L A T E A U

• Brasília

• La Paz

Galápagos Islands

About 600 miles (960 kilometers) off the coast of northwestern South America lies a group of volcanic islands known as the Galápagos. They are part of the nation of Ecuador, and there are thirteen main islands in the group. Though they fall right on the equator, the islands lie in the path of a cold current, so their climate is generally cooler and drier than the climate of other equatorial regions.

ATACAMA DESERT

ANDES

GRAN CHACO

Paraguay R.

PARAGUAY

Asunción •

São Paulo •

• Rio de Janeiro

Tropic of Capricorn

Iguaçu
Falls

Paraná River

A R G E N T I N A

C H I L E

• Córdoba

Santiago •

▲ Mount
Aconcagua

URUGUAY

Atlantic Ocean

Buenos Aires •

Río de la Plata

• Montevideo

PAMPA

P A T A G O N I A

0   300   600 Mi.

0   300   600 Km.

Scale

FALKLAND
ISLANDS

Cape Horn

Rain Forest

The South American rain forest was once broken only by the muddy red course of the Amazon and its tributaries. There is no change of seasons here—it is always rainy and hot. The water from the leaves and the tangles of vines create a dank environment under the trees that steams in constant heat. The rain forest crawls with life from the top to bottom, with different animals adapting to life at different levels.

Hundreds of species of colorful birds fill the trees; toucans and parrots sometimes grapple with their large bills. Spider monkeys and howler monkeys call loudly to one another and swing with the aid of their tails. Unlike their relatives in other parts of the world, some South American monkeys can wrap their tails around tree branches. The largest of all snakes, the anaconda, slithers among the trees and reaches lengths of up to thirty-five feet (about eleven meters). In the waters of the forest live the fierce flesh-eating piranha and the caiman, a relative of the alligator. Electric eels lurk in the depths, shocking their prey with volts of electricity.

Today, the rain forest is in danger. Huge portions of it are being cleared. Many experts fear this is causing extreme damage to the wildlife here and to world ecology.

Macaws live in the highest branches of the forest, where few predators can reach. The birds' main enemies are people who catch them to sell as pets. The hyacinth macaw, for example, may become extinct for this reason.

The golden lion tamarin is one of the rarest monkeys in South America. It, too, has become endangered as a result of capture for the pet industry. Only about four hundred live in the wild, in a Brazilian preserve.

Like other constrictors, boa constrictors kill their prey by wrapping around it and squeezing, thereby suffocating it. Boas are not poisonous, however, and will usually flee when encountered by humans.

Jaguars resemble leopards but are slightly larger. They are the only big cats in South America. Nocturnal animals of the dense Amazonian forest include huge, hairy tarantulas and blood-sucking vampire bats. Though fearsome, these animals are rarely dangerous to humans. Sloths are among the largest and most widespread of South American mammals.

Gran Chaco and Pampa

Grasses and low-growing shrubs spread out under the vast sky in the Gran Chaco. This is the home of the maned wolf and several types of armadillos. For example, the giant armadillo lives here. It is a heavily armored beast that might weigh over a hundred pounds (forty-five kilograms). An armadillo may look fearsome, but it is shy and will curl up into a ball if provoked. The marshes of the Gran Chaco, near the Paraguay River, are the home of a large number of waterfowl.

The Pampa is an ocean of grasses, broken occasionally by umbrella-shaped trees. The Pampa is drier near the Andes in the west and wetter near the Atlantic in the east. The guanaco, a widespread relative of the llama, ranges far and wide, feeding on the plants of the Pampa. Guanacos once shared the grasses with a large number of Pampas deer, but there are now very few deer left. The cavy and its close relative the mara also live here.

The greatest threat to wildlife here is the farmer. Lands are being cleared to grow crops and to raise cattle. Grazing wild animals must compete with cattle for food. Predators who might feed on cattle are killed off. All wildlife here is losing its habitat to plowed fields and fenced pastures.

Maned wolves look more like foxes on stilts than they do wolves. They are a vulnerable species. Guinea pigs, which are popular pets, were bred from cavies, the most common rodents in South America. The Pampas deer is an endangered species, a victim of hunting and loss of habitat. The Chacoan peccary is a member of the pig family, and it, too, is vulnerable.

The common rhea of the Pampa grows over five feet (about one and one-half meters) tall. Rheas cannot fly, but they can outrun a horse. Loss of habitat to farmland has forced rheas from their homes and reduced their numbers.

The largest rodents in the world, capybaras can stand up to two feet (about one-half meter) tall at the shoulder and weigh more than a hundred pounds (forty-five kilograms). Capybaras always live near water. They have webbed feet and are good swimmers.

Andes

High in the Andes, the climates and habitats change—and so do the animals. At the bottom of the mountains are tropical forests. The middle zones are temperate or cool. In these low and middle zones, such animals as ocelots and coatis are found. At the very peaks, the air is very thin, the landscape is very rocky and rugged, and the climate is very harsh. Here only the hardiest of plants and animals can survive.

Three of the animals of the Andes are related to one another and to the camels of Africa and Asia. Llamas and alpacas are two of these animals. Today, all llamas and alpacas are domesticated, but they once roamed wild in the middle altitudes of the mountains. Vicuñas, the smallest and rarest of the three, live only in the high grasslands found above twelve thousand feet (thirty-six hundred meters).

At the greatest heights of the Andes, over fifteen thousand feet (forty-five hundred meters), only the most resourceful of birds can live. Some of these small birds have been nicknamed "miners," because they dig burrows in the ground to protect them from the harsh climate. This is also the realm of the Andean condor.

Colorful torrent ducks brave the cold, fast-flowing streams of the high Andes. The Andean condor, a member of the vulture family, is one of the world's largest birds. Its strength and flying skill allow it to fly high into the peaks, where most animals cannot go. White markings on the faces of spectacled bears have given them their name. They are the only bears in South America.

A few years ago, vicuñas, which are valued for their fine wool, were endangered. Since becoming protected, their numbers have increased. Most vicuñas live in Peru, but they are also found in Ecuador and Bolivia.

Humans tamed the sturdy, woolly llama as long as four thousand years ago. Today all llamas are domesticated. Millions of llamas are kept by humans in the Andes, mainly for transportation and for wool.

Galápagos Islands

Rocky, hardened lava beds, several types of cactus, and a strange procession of wildlife characterize these remote islands. Never were they part of any mainland, having been formed by volcanoes on the ocean floor. So far away from any major land region are they that few animals reached them of their own accord. Those that did—mainly reptiles, birds, and sea creatures—developed in unique ways. In many cases, the same animal appears with variations on several different islands. In the 1830s, the naturalist Charles Darwin, who was visiting the islands, noted these variations among species. This observation contributed to his theory of evolution.

Key to Darwin's theory was his study of the finches of the Galápagos. Fifteen species of these birds appear, each with a slightly different feeding niche and a bill that is shaped to allow it to exploit its niche.

Many of the unique creatures of the Galápagos are in danger. Many have been overhunted by humans. But people are not the only predators—domestic animals take their toll on the wildlife as well. Competition for food between wild and domestic creatures is also a problem.

The rare marine iguana of the Galápagos is the only lizard that regularly swims in water. It eats algae, which it finds along the shore and on the ocean floor. Marine iguanas can be four feet (over one meter) long.

Crabs of the Galápagos share the shoreline with marine iguanas. These crabs sometimes walk across the bodies of basking iguanas, pulling ticks from the iguanas' skins and eating them.

A skilled predator, the Galápagos hawk is a threat to the domestic animals owned by people who have settled the islands. As a result, many of these birds have been killed, and today the Galápagos hawk is a rare species.

The rare flightless cormorant had few enemies until such domestic predators as dogs and cats arrived. Aside from the Galápagos hawk, the land iguana had little to fear either. This iguana may exist near the marine iguana, but it does not swim. Today, the land iguana is a vulnerable species. The shells of Galápagos tortoises, also a vulnerable species, vary from one island to another.

Polar Regions

Around the North Pole is the region known as the Arctic. The Arctic is often defined as the area that falls within the Arctic Circle. It is a region that includes the Arctic Ocean, many islands, the northern parts of Europe, Asia, and North America, and most of Greenland. Antarctica, at the South Pole, is a land mass that is larger than Europe or Australia. Most of the continent of Antarctica falls within the Antarctic Circle, another imaginary line.

The Arctic

North of the Arctic Circle, the sun does not set for one or more days a year. It stays above the horizon on the longest days of the year, which occur in June. It does not rise at all on the shortest days of the year, which fall in December. The Arctic is blanketed with ice and snow for much of the year. It is too cold and desolate for humans and most animals. Almost all the ice and snow melt, however, when summer comes.

Antarctica

The same phenomenon of the never-setting and never-rising sun occurs south of the Antarctic Circle, except in opposite seasons. Here the shortest days are in June and the longest are in December. Unlike the Arctic, much of Antarctica is covered with permanent ice and snow. Surrounding the South Pole is the loneliest, most bitterly cold region on earth. The temperatures here fall much lower than they ever do at the North Pole. Antarctica is one of the world's last frontiers. It has no permanent human population, and thus no government. Many nations have claimed parts of Antarctica.

ASIA

90° E   60° E

Circle

Ob River

URAL MTS.

ET UNION

EUROPE

30° E

Barents
Sea

FINLAND

SVALBARD

SWEDEN

Norwegian
Sea

NORWAY

North Pole

Arctic Ocean

GREENLAND

30° W

QUEEN

ELIZABETH

ISLANDS

60° W

RTH

Arctic Circle

RICA

Hudson
Bay

ADA

180°

90° W

90° W

120° W

150° W

Pacific Ocean

Amundsen
Sea

ANTARCTIC
PENINSULA

60° W

Weddell
Sea

30° W

Ross
Sea

0°

ROSS
ICE
SHELF

MOUNTAINS

South Pole

TRANSANTARCTIC

ANTARCTICA

150° E

AMERICAN
HIGHLAND

30° E

120° E

90° E

Antarctic Circle

60° E

Indian Ocean

©1990 Rand McNally & Co.

Scale

0   300   600 Mi.

0   300   600 Km.

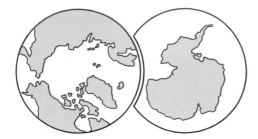

The Arctic and Antarctica

Much life of the Arctic appears in the seas, which warm up during summer months. The frozen surfaces of the winter ice cap are relatively free of creatures, except maybe an occasional walrus, seal, or polar bear. In spring the Arctic *tundra*, or plain, blossoms with life. Here such creatures as musk oxen, reindeer, wolves, and lemmings are found. The coasts are crowded with birds spending their summers here.

In contrast to the Arctic, the temperatures of most of Antarctica always stay well below freezing. In the interior, the climate is so harsh that neither humans nor animals are able to withstand it. Only along the seacoasts, where the waters have a warming effect, are many animals found. Several species of seals and penguins inhabit these coasts. The waters off the Antarctic coasts are the realm of many whales.

Many creatures of the polar regions are killed for their thick, warm furs and for such items as oils and tusks. The exploitation of natural resources in the polar regions damages animal habitats. The drilling and transport of oil in the Arctic, for example, has resulted in oil leaks and spills that have killed millions of animals.

The polar bear is the largest carnivorous animal that lives on land. Never straying far from water, its main prey is seals. Polar bears are a vulnerable species and inhabit the waters and coasts around the North Pole.

Puffins come ashore only to nest, spending most of their lives on the open seas. When puffins do nest, they do so in burrows that they dig along the coasts of northern Europe, Greenland, and North America.

Penguins are a common sight on the lands and in the waters surrounding the South Pole. However, the adelie penguin, shown here, and the emperor penguin are the only species that nest on the continent of Antarctica.

The coat of the Arctic fox changes with the seasons. In summer, it is a dull gray; in winter, it turns white. The color of the snowy owl's feathers similarly changes. Musk oxen, with their shaggy, thick wool coats, are well suited to life in the Arctic. Caribou and reindeer were once considered two different animals. Today they are classified as a single species.

Oceans

The oceans of the world are linked together to form one continuous area of salt water that covers more than 70 percent of the earth. The continental land areas separate this huge body of water into distinct oceans. Other large bodies of salt water, some called seas or gulfs, are also part of the world ocean. Coral reefs, made up of living coral formations, are found in warm ocean waters around the world.

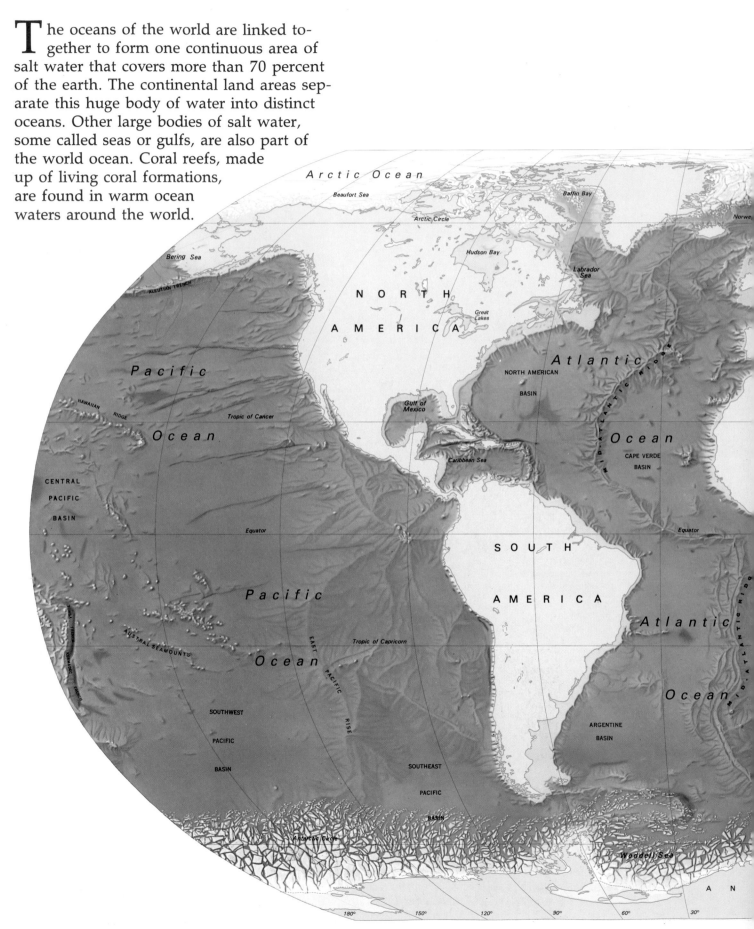

Arctic Ocean

Beaufort Sea

Baffin Bay

Arctic Circle

Norwe

Bering Sea

Hudson Bay

Labrador Sea

ALEUTIAN TRENCH

NORTH

AMERICA

Great Lakes

Atlantic

Pacific

NORTH AMERICAN

BASIN

HAWAIIAN RIDGE

Ocean

Tropic of Cancer

Gulf of Mexico

Ocean

CAPE VERDE

BASIN

CENTRAL

PACIFIC

BASIN

Caribbean Sea

Equator

Equator

SOUTH

Pacific

AMERICA

Atlantic

AUSTRAL SEAMOUNTS

TONGA TRENCH

KERMADEC TRENCH

Ocean

EAST PACIFIC

Tropic of Capricorn

Tropic of Capricorn

Ocean

SOUTHWEST

PACIFIC

RISE

ARGENTINE

BASIN

BASIN

SOUTHEAST

PACIFIC

BASIN

Antarctic Circle

Weddell Sea

A N

180°   150°   120°   90°   60°   30°

Open Sea

The oceans of the world are the Atlantic, Pacific, Indian, and Arctic. Major seas include the Mediterranean, Arabian, and Caribbean. The Gulf of Mexico is another major body of salt water. The floor of the ocean has features just like land does. Ridges, basins, and trenches are a few of the features.

Coral Reef

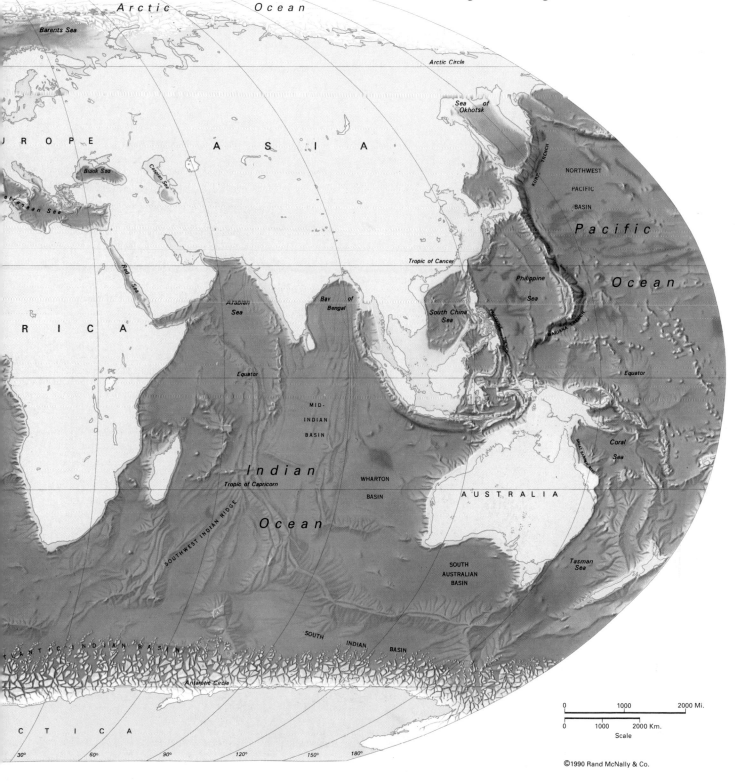

Coral reefs are found in many undersea regions around the world. The major reef regions are in the Caribbean Sea and the Indian and Pacific oceans, between the Tropic of Cancer and the Tropic of Capricorn. The Great Barrier Reef, off the northeastern coast of Australia, is over one thousand miles (sixteen hundred kilometers) long, making it the largest coral reef in the world.

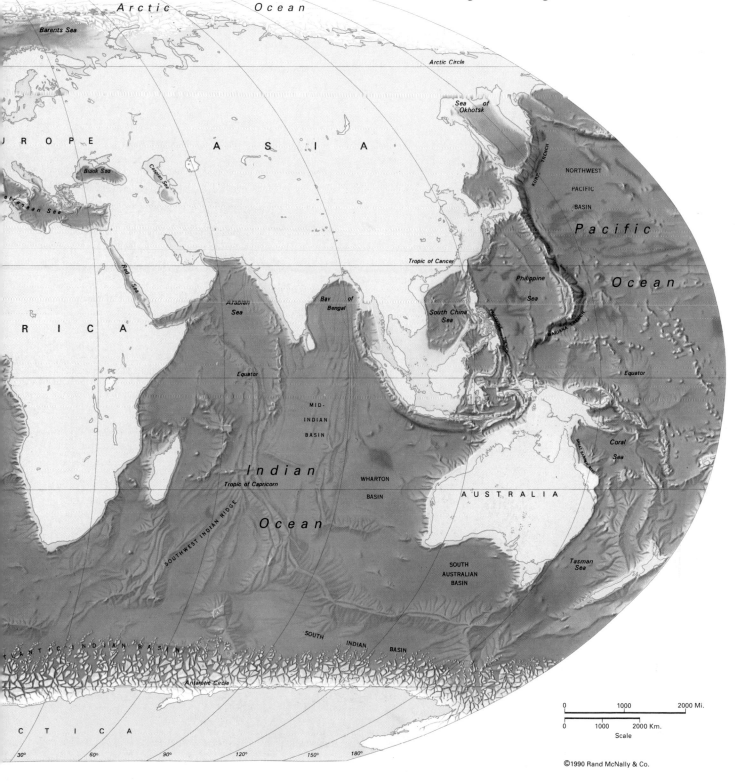

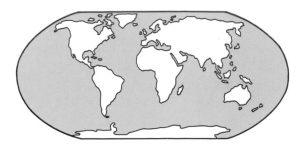

Open Sea

In the world's oceans, the food chain is much the same as it is on land. Life is based on plants, which are eaten by herbivores, which are eaten by carnivores, which are then eaten by larger carnivores, and so on. At the bottom of the chain is plankton, the smallest plants and animals of the deep. At the top of the chain are predators such as sharks.

Different types of marine life have adapted to life at various depths. Near the surface, where the water is lighted and warmed by the sun, the greatest number of creatures live. This is the realm of the most familiar fishes. Herrings and sardines live in great groups, or *schools*, while sharks and whales swim alone. Farther down, the fish become more unusual as they have adapted to cold temperatures and poor lighting. The organs of the hatchet fish, for example, glow in the murky waters of the middle

Most rays, such as these eagle rays, inhabit warm waters. Eagle rays have poisonous spines, which trail behind them. The ray family includes manta rays, which can be twenty feet (six meters) across.

The eight-armed octopus is a carnivorous *mollusk* found in almost all oceans. Octopuses have highly developed brains and nervous systems and are considered intelligent. Some species may span thirty feet (nine meters).

depths. At the very bottom lurks the deep-sea angler, a strange creature that possesses a glowing spiny ray, which it uses to attract prey.

For many years, humans have used the ocean as a dumping ground, and some people fear that the effects of all the pollution are only just beginning to show.

Gulls are a familiar seaside sight. With more than eighty species, gulls are found all over the world. Like many types of birds, most gulls are *migratory*; that is, they fly to different areas during different seasons.

The albatross spends most of its life out on the open sea, especially in the Southern Hemisphere. Whales and dolphins are warm-blooded, intelligent mammals. Both have suffered greatly at the hands of hunters and fishermen. So has the leatherback, the largest of sea turtles. Sharks appear worldwide and with great variety—there are approximately 350 species of sharks.

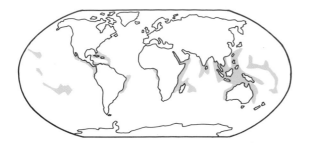

Coral Reef

In tropical regions around the world, coral reefs appear like three-dimensional, patterned carpets on the ocean floor. The living corals rise up in intricate shapes, harboring an incredible variety and number of brilliantly colored sea creatures. Coral reefs have been compared with rain forests because both are inhabited by a very large number of species.

Coral may form less than half of the reef. Various algae make up an important part of the reef. Starfish and sea urchins feed on coral and algae and are often found in the reef habitat. Giant clams, shrimp, and crabs live here as well. But the most spectacular residents of the reef are the stunning varieties of fish that flit among the corals, creating an ever-changing rainbow of color.

Environmentalists are concerned about coral reefs. Pollution in the world's oceans can wipe out reefs. Coral reefs are especially vulnerable because they so frequently occur close to shore, where there is a greater concentration of pollution. Corals are mined for building materials, jewelry, and other goods. As a result, some reefs have been destroyed.

Corals are living animals that form the foundation of the reef. Many other animals contribute to the reef habitat. Sea anemones appear in several different forms, and some attach themselves to corals. Colorful angelfish and triggerfish are commonly found near reefs; the triggerfish is the largest fish shown here. Hiding among the corals are eels, which dart out to catch their prey.

Perhaps more feared than sharks, barracudas can grow up to ten feet (three meters) long. They inhabit temperate and tropical waters and can be dangerous to humans if provoked.

The zebra-striped lionfish is common in coral reefs of the Indian and Pacific oceans. The spines of the lionfish are venomous and provide defense against would-be predators.

Glossary

Alpine   A word used to describe regions with high mountains.

Arid   A word used to describe areas with very little rainfall. A dry and barren area with very little moisture.

Broadleaf   Another word for *deciduous*.

Capercaillie   A plump game bird with strong feathered legs. It usually has reddish brown or some other protective coloring.

Captivity   To be kept under the control of another. Animals are tamed and kept under the control of humans.

Carcass   The body of a dead animal.

Carnivorous   Any kind of animal that mainly eats the flesh of other animals. A word to describe meat-eating animals.

Coniferous   A type of tree or shrub that bears cones and is usually evergreen. Pine, spruce, and fir trees are conifers.

Cordillera   A long mountain range or a chain of mountains.

Deciduous   A type of tree or shrub that sheds its leaves each year. Maple, oak, and elm trees are deciduous.

Deforestation   The act of removing trees or forests to clear the land.

Desert   A dry, barren region that is usually covered with sand or rocks in which few plants and animals live. Deserts can be hot or cold.

Edelweiss   A small plant that grows in high places with heads of very small white flowers in the center of star-shaped leaf clusters.

Endangered   A word to describe a species that is in danger becoming extinct unless action is taken to preserve it.

Eucalyptus   A very tall evergreen tree that grows mainly in Australia and neighboring islands.

Extinct   A word to describe a species that has not been definitely sighted in the wild in the last fifty years.

Feline   Any catlike, meat-eating animal including domestic cats, lions, tigers, and panthers.

Habitat   A place where animals or plants naturally grow and live.

Herbivore   Any kind of animal that mainly eats plants. A word to describe plant-eating animals.

Hibernate   To spend the winter in sleep or in some other inactive condition.

Indeterminate   A word to describe a species known to be either endangered, vulnerable, or rare, but not enough is known to classify it exactly.

Insufficiently known   A word to describe a species that is suspected of being at risk but not enough is known about it to assign a definite category.

Mammal   A warm-blooded animal that feeds milk to its young and is usually covered with hair.

Marsupial   A type of mammal that carries its young in a pouch on the outside of the mother's body.

Migration   The act of moving from one place to another. The act of going from one region to another with the change in the seasons, often looking for food.

Mollusk   Any type of animal having a soft body not made up of segments and usually covered with a hard shell. A type of shellfish.

Monsoon   A periodic wind with heavy rainfall. A word most often associated with this type of weather as it occurs in India and nearby areas.

Needleleaf   Another word for *coniferous*.

Nocturnal   A word to describe an animal that is most active at night and sleeps during the day.

Omnivorous   Any kind of animal that eats any kind of food including meat and plants. A word to describe meat- and plant-eating animals.

Plumage   The feathers of a bird.

Poacher   A person who catches or kills animals illegally.

Predator   A type of animal that lives by hunting and killing other animals for food.

Prehensile   A word to describe something that is capable of seizing, grasping, and hanging on. Very often used to describe tails of animals.

Pride   A group of lions made up of one to five adult males, several females, and cubs or young lions.

Primate   A group of mammals that have very advanced brains. Primates have hands with thumbs that can grasp things. Apes, monkeys, and human beings are primates.

Range   A word that describes the area in which a certain animal may be found. Several habitats may be included in the range of a species.

Rare   A word to describe a species with a small population that is at risk but is not presently endangered or vulnerable.

Rhododendron   An evergreen shrub with glossy, oval leaves and clusters of large pink, purple, or white flowers.

Savanna   A grassy plain with few or no trees.

Scavenger   A type of animal that eats dead, decaying, or rotting animal or plant matter.

School   A large group of the same kind of fish or water animals swimming together.

Species   A group of animals that have enough in common so they can be designated by the same name.

Steppe   A vast, treeless plain, especially in southeastern Europe and Asia.

Taiga   A moist, cold, coniferous forest near the edge of a tundra.

Temperate   A word that describes weather that is not very hot and not very cold; moderate; not having extremes.

Terrain   A tract or stretch of land considered with respect to its natural features.

Threatened   A general term that is used to describe species that are somehow at risk.

Treeline   The upper limit of tree growth in mountains and other high altitudes. Also called *timberline*.

Tributary   A stream or river that flows into a larger stream, river, or other body of water.

Tundra   A vast, level, treeless plain in arctic or very cold regions.

Venomous   A word that describes an animal capable of secreting poison or venom.

Vulnerable   A word to describe a species that is likely to become endangered in the near future unless action is taken to preserve it.

Selected Threatened Animals

Following are some of the most familiar of the world's threatened species. Animals are listed first by region, then in alphabetic order by name. The official status of each animal is also stated. See the glossary for the meaning of each status. If an animal lives in more than one region, it is listed under the region in which it appears in this atlas.

Europe

Abruzzo chamois, vulnerable, Italy

Barbary macaque, vulnerable, Algeria, Gibraltar, Morocco

Chartreuse chamois, endangered, France

Cyprus mouflon, vulnerable, Cyprus

European bison, vulnerable, Soviet Union, Poland

Loggerhead turtle, vulnerable, subtropical and temperate seas

Mediterranean monk seal, endangered, Mediterranean and Mauritanian coasts

Pyrenean desman, vulnerable, France, Portugal, Spain

Pyrenean ibex, endangered, Spain

Sardinian mouflon, vulnerable, Sardinia, Corsica

Asia

Asian elephant, endangered, Asia

Asiatic lion, endangered, India

Asiatic water buffalo, endangered, India, Nepal

Asiatic wild ass, vulnerable, Asia

Bactrian camel, vulnerable, China, Mongolia

Clouded leopard, vulnerable, Asia

Dugong, vulnerable, Coastal Indian and Western Pacific Oceans

Ganges River dolphin, vulnerable, India, Bangladesh, Nepal, Bhutan

Gharial, endangered, South Asia

Giant panda, rare, China

Gray wolf, vulnerable, North America, Middle East, Eurasia

Indian python, vulnerable, Southern Asia

Indus River dolphin, endangered, Pakistan

Komodo dragon, rare, Indonesia

Malayan tapir, endangered, Southeast Asia

Markhor, vulnerable, West Himalayas

Orang-utan, endangered, Borneo, Sumatra

Philippine tarsier, endangered, Philippines

Proboscis monkey, vulnerable, Borneo

Przewalski's horse, extinct?, China, Mongolia

Red panda, insufficiently known, Nepal to China

Snow leopard, endangered, Asia

Tiger, endangered, Asia

Yak, endangered, Central Asia

Africa

Addax, endangered, Sahara, Sahel

African elephant, endangered, Africa

African wild dog, vulnerable, Subsaharan Africa

Aye-aye, endangered, Madagascar

Barbary sheep, vulnerable, Sahara, Sahel

Black rhinoceros, endangered, Africa

Cheetah, vulnerable, Africa, Middle East, Iran, Soviet Union

Chimpanzee, vulnerable, Equatorial Africa

Gorilla, vulnerable, Equatorial Africa

Grevy's zebra, endangered, Ethiopia, Kenya, Somalia

Leopard, threatened, Africa, Middle East, Asia

Mandrill, vulnerable, Cameroon, Congo, Equatorial Guinea, Gabon

Mountain gorilla, endangered, Rwanda, Uganda, Zaire

Ring-tailed lemur, insufficiently known, Madagascar

Ruffed lemur, indeterminate, Madagascar

Scimitar-horned oryx, endangered, Sahara, Sahel

Web-footed tenrec, vulnerable, Madagascar

Zanzibar bush baby, insufficiently known, East Africa

Oceania

Blue bird of paradise, vulnerable, New Guinea

Cuscus, rare, New Guinea

Kakapo, endangered, New Zealand

Long-beaked echidna, vulnerable, New Guinea

Northern hairy-nosed wombat, endangered, Australia

Numbat, endangered, Australia

Tuatara, rare, New Zealand

Samoan flying fox, endangered, Samoa, Fiji Islands

Victoria crowned pigeon, insufficiently known, New Guinea, Indonesia

Western barred bandicoot, rare, Australia

North America

California condor, endangered, United States

Crested honeycreeper, vulnerable, Hawaii

Gila monster, vulnerable, Mexico, United States

Hawaiian goose, vulnerable, Hawaii

Hawaiian monk seal, endangered, Hawaii

Indiana bat, vulnerable, United States

Key deer, rare, United States

Margay cat, vulnerable, Central and South America

Ocelot, vulnerable, United States, Central and South America

Red wolf, endangered, United States

Resplendent quetzal, vulnerable, Central America

Utah prairie dog, vulnerable, United States

Whooping crane, endangered, Canada, United States

Wolverine, vulnerable, Eurasia, North America

South America

Amazon River dolphin, vulnerable, South America

Argentinian pampas deer, endangered, Argentina

Chacoan peccary, vulnerable, Argentina, Bolivia, Paraguay

Galápagos flightless cormorant, rare, Galápagos

Galápagos giant tortoise, vulnerable, Galápagos

Galápagos hawk, rare, Galápagos

Galápagos land iguana, vulnerable, Galápagos

Galápagos marine iguana, rare, Galápagos

Giant armadillo, vulnerable, South America

Golden lion tamarin, endangered, Brazil

Jaguar, vulnerable, United States, Central and South America

Long-tailed chinchilla, indeterminate, Chile

Maned sloth, endangered, Brazil

Maned wolf, vulnerable, South America

Short-tailed chinchilla, indeterminate, Andes

Spectacled bear, vulnerable, South America

Vicuña, vulnerable, Andes

Woolly monkey, vulnerable, South America

Polar Regions

Narwhal, insufficiently known, Arctic Ocean

Polar bear, vulnerable, Arctic

Oceans

Blue whale, endangered, all oceans

Fin whale, vulnerable, all oceans

Humpback whale, endangered, all oceans

Leatherback, endangered, tropical and temperate seas

Selected National Parks and Protected Areas

Following are some of the largest of the world's national parks and other protected areas. Abbreviations are as follows: GR = Game Reserve, MP = Marine Park, NM = National Monument, NP = National Park, P = Park, PP = Provincial Park, WA = Wilderness Area, WS = Wildlife Sanctuary. The parks are listed first by region, then in alphabetic order by country, and finally in alphabetic order by name.

Europe

Lemmenjoen NP, Finland
Urho Kekkosen NP, Finland
Borgefjell NP, Norway
Hardangervidda NP, Norway

Jotunheimen NP, Norway
Northwest Spitzbergen NP, Norway
Ovre Anarjokka NP, Norway

South Spitzbergen NP, Norway
Padjelanta NP, Sweden
Sareks NP, Sweden

Asia

Jigme Dorji WS, Bhutan
Desert NP, India
Great Himalayan NP, India
Indravati NP, India
Namdapha NP, India
Panna NP, India
Sunderbans NP, India
Barisan Selatan NP, Indonesia
Dumoga-Bone NP, Indonesia
Gunung Leuser NP, Indonesia
Kepulauan Seribu NP, Indonesia
Kerinci Seblat NP, Indonesia

Kutai NP, Indonesia
Lore Lindu NP, Indonesia
Manusela Wai Nua/Wai Mual NP, Indonesia
Morowali NP, Indonesia
Tanjung Puting NP, Indonesia
Central Alborz, Iran
Golestan NP, Iran
Kavir, Iran
Lake Oromeeh, Iran
Crocker Range NP, Malaysia

Endau Rompin NP, Malaysia
Taman Negara NP, Malaysia
Great Gobi Desert NP, Mongolia
Langtang NP, Nepal
Sagarmatha NP, Nepal
Shey-Phoksundo NP, Nepal
Khunjerab NP, Pakistan
Asir NP, Saudi Arabia
Sevan NP, Soviet Union
Wilpattu NP, Sri Lanka
Khao Yai NP, Thailand

Africa

Tassili N'Ajjer NP, Algeria
Boucle de las Pendjari, Benin
"W" du Benin, Benin
Chobe NP, Botswana
Gemsbok NP, Botswana
Po NP, Burkina Faso
"W" du Burkina Faso, Burkina Faso
Benoue NP, Cameroon
Boubandjidah NP, Cameroon
Faro NP, Cameroon
Waza NP, Cameroon
Bamingui-Bangoran NP, Central African Republic
Manovo-Gounda-Saint Floris NP, Central African Republic
Manda NP, Chad
Odzala NP, Congo

Bale Mountains NP, Ethiopia
Omo NP, Ethiopia
Bui NP, Ghana
Digya NP, Ghana
Mole NP, Ghana
Komoe NP, Ivory Coast
Marahoue NP, Ivory Coast
Tai NP, Ivory Coast
Marsabit NP, Kenya
Masai Mara GR, Kenya
Sibiloi NP, Kenya
Tsavo NP, Kenya
Sapo NP, Liberia
Kasungu NP, Malawi
Nyika NP, Malawi
Boucle du Baoule NP, Mali
Banc d'Arguin, Mauritania

Banhine NP, Mozambique
Gorongosa NP, Mozambique
Zinave NP, Mozambique
Etosha NP, Namibia
Namib/Naukluft Park, Namibia
Skeleton Coast Park, Namibia
"W" du Niger, Niger
Kainji Lake NP, Nigeria
Akagera NP, Rwanda
Niokolo Koba NP, Senegal
Lag Badana NP, Somalia
Kalahari Gemsbok NP, South Africa
Kruger NP, South Africa
Dinder NP, Sudan
Radom NP, Sudan
Katavi NP, Tanzania
Mikumi NP, Tanzania

Ruaha NP, Tanzania
Serengeti NP, Tanzania
Tarangire NP, Tanzania
Fazao NP, Togo
Keran NP, Togo
Kabalega NP, Uganda
Kidepo Valley NP, Uganda
Queen Elizabeth NP, Uganda
Garamba NP, Zaire
Kahuzi-Biega NP, Zaire
Kundelungu NP, Zaire

Maiko NP, Zaire
Salonga NP, Zaire
Upemba NP, Zaire
Virunga NP, Zaire
Kafue NP, Zambia
Lavushi Manda NP, Zambia
Liuwa Plain NP, Zambia
Lower Zambezi NP, Zambia
Lukusuzi NP, Zambia
Mweru Mantipa NP, Zambia
North Luangwa NP, Zambia

Nyika NP, Zambia
Sioma Ngweze NP, Zambia
South Luangwa NP, Zambia
Sumbu NP, Zambia
West Lunga NP, Zambia
Chizarira NP, Zimbabwe
Gonarezhou NP, Zimbabwe
Hwange NP, Zimbabwe
Mana Pools NP, Zimbabwe
Matusadona NP, Zimbabwe

Oceania

Archer Bend NP, Australia
Blue Mountains NP, Australia
Cape Arid NP, Australia
Carnarvon NP, Australia
Collier Range NP, Australia
Cradle Mountain-Lake St. Clair NP,
   Australia
Drysdale River NP, Australia
Fitzgerald River NP, Australia
Franklin-Lower Gordon Wild Rivers
   NP, Australia
Gammon Ranges NP, Australia
Grampians NP, Australia
Great Barrier Reef MP, Australia

Gurig NP, Australia
Hamersley Range NP, Australia
Jardine River NP, Australia
Kakadu NP, Australia
Kalbarri NP, Australia
Katherine Gorge NP, Australia
Kosciusko NP, Australia
Lakefield NP, Australia
McIllwraith Range NP, Australia
Millstream Chichester Range NP,
   Australia
Morton NP, Australia
Nullarbor NP, Australia
Rokeby NP, Australia

Rudall River NP, Australia
Simpson Desert NP, Australia
Southwest NP, Australia
Staaten River NP, Australia
Stirling Range NP, Australia
Sturt NP, Australia
Wollemi NP, Australia
Wonnangatta-Moroka NP, Australia
Wyperfield NP, Australia
Fiordland NP, New Zealand
Mount Aspiring NP, New Zealand
Urewera NP, New Zealand
Westland NP, New Zealand

North America

Algonquin PP, Canada
Atlin PP, Canada
Auyuittug NP, Canada
Avalon WA, Canada
Banff NP, Canada
Gaspesie PP, Canada
Glacier NP, Canada
Gros Morne NP, Canada
Jasper NP, Canada
Kluane NP, Canada
Kootenay NP, Canada
Kwadacha Wilderness P, Canada
Lake Superior PP, Canada
Laurentides, Canada
Mont Tremblant NP, Canada
Mount Edziza P, Canada
Mount Robson PP, Canada
Nahanni NP, Canada
Northern Yukon NP, Canada
Polar Bear PP, Canada
Prince Albert NP, Canada
Pukaskwa NP, Canada
Quetico NP, Canada

Riding Mountain NP, Canada
Spatsizi Plateau Wilderness, Canada
Strathcona PP, Canada
Tatlutai PP, Canada
Tweedsmuir PP, Canada
Wells Gray PP, Canada
Wood Buffalo NP, Canada
Yoho NP, Canada
Cordillera de Talamanca NP, Costa Rica
Greenland NP, Greenland
Rio Platano, Honduras
Darien NP, Panama
Aniakchak NM, United States
Bering Land Bridge National Preserve,
   United States
Big Bend NP, United States
Canyonlands NP, United States
Cape Krusenstern NM, United States
Death Valley NM, United States
Denali NP, United States
Everglades NP, United States
Gates of the Arctic NP, United States
Glacier Bay NP, United States

Glacier NP, United States
Grand Canyon NP, United States
Grand Teton NP, United States
Great Smoky Mountains NP, United
   States
Isle Royale NP, United States
Joshua Tree NM, United States
Katmai NP, United States
Kenai Fjords NP, United States
Kings Canyon NP, United States
Kobuk Valley NP, United States
Lake Clark NP, United States
Noatak National Preserve, United
   States
North Cascades NP, United States
Olympic NP, United States
Organ Pipe Cactus NM, United States
Rocky Mountain NP, United States
Sequoia NP, United States
Wrangell-St. Elias NP, United States
Yellowstone NP, United States
Yosemite NP, United States
Yukon Charley NM, United States

South America

Alerces NP, Argentina
Lanin NP, Argentina
Los Glaciares NP, Argentina
Nahuel Huapi NP, Argentina
Amboro NP, Bolivia
Huanchaca NP, Bolivia
Isiboro Secure NP, Bolivia
Amazonia NP, Brazil
Araguaia NP, Brazil
Cabo Orange NP, Brazil
Emas NP, Brazil
Iguacu NP, Brazil
Jau NP, Brazil
Lencois Maranhenses NP, Brazil
Pacaas Novos NP, Brazil
Pantanal Matogrossense NP, Brazil
Pico da Neblina NP, Brazil
Serra da Bocaina NP, Brazil
Serra da Capivara NP, Brazil
Alberto de Angostini NP, Chile
Bernardo O'Higgins NP, Chile
Hernando de Magellanes NP, Chile

Isla Magdalena NP, Chile
Laguna San Rafael NP, Chile
Lauca NP, Chile
Puyehue NP, Chile
Quelat NP, Chile
Torres del Paine NP, Chile
Vicente Perez Rosales NP, Chile
Volcan Isluga NP, Chile
Amacayacu NP, Colombia
Cordillera de los Picachos NP,
  Colombia
El Cocuy NP, Colombia
El Tuparro NP, Colombia
Farallones de Cali NP, Colombia
Nevado del Huila NP, Colombia
Paramillo NP, Colombia
Paramo de las Hermosas NP, Colombia
Sierra de la Macarena NP, Colombia
Sierra Nevada de Santa Maria NP,
  Colombia
Sumapaz NP, Colombia

Galápagos NP, Ecuador
Podocarpus NP, Ecuador
Sangay NP, Ecuador
Yasuni NP, Ecuador
Defensores del Chaco NP, Paraguay
Tinfunque NP, Paraguay
Huascaran NP, Peru
Manu NP, Peru
Pampas del Heath NP, Peru
Rio Abiseo NP, Peru
Aguaro-Guariquito NP, Venezuela
Archipelago los Roques NP, Venezuela
Canaima NP, Venezuela
Duida-Marahuaca NP, Venezuela
El Tama NP, Venezuela
Henry Pittier NP, Venezuela
Jaua-Sarisarinama NP, Venezuela
Perija NP, Venezuela
Serrania de la Neblina NP, Venezuela
Sierra Nevada NP, Venezuela
Yacapana NP, Venezuela

Subject Index

Numbers in *italics* refer to illustrations or photographs.

A
Addax 36
Albatross 76
Algae 78
Alligator 57
Alpaca 66
Anaconda 62
Anemone, sea 79
Angelfish 78
Ant, driver 34
Anteater 59
Antelope 32
Armadillo 59; giant 64
Ass, Asian wild 20, 20
Aye-aye 40, 40

B
Badger 12, 22
Bandicoot 46, 47
Bat 28; flying fox 29; vampire 63
Bear, Asian black 22; black 57; brown 20; grizzly 52, 53; polar 72; spectacled 67
Beaver 52
Bird of paradise 44, 45
Bison 55
Boa constrictor 63
Boar 12, 13, 22, 23
Bobcat 54
Bongo 34
Budgerigar 47
Buffalo, water 27
Bullfrog 57
Bush baby 35
Butterfly, swallowtail 22

C
Caiman 62
Camel 36, 37; Bactrian 20, 21
Capercaillie 14
Capybara 65
Caribou 73
Cat, Margay 58, 59; tiger 48
Cassowary 44
Cavy 64, 64

Chameleon 40, 40
Chamois 15
Cheetah 32, 33
Chevrotain 34
Chicken, prairie 54
Cichlid 38
Chimpanzee 34
Chipmunk 20, 52, 56
Civet 26
Clam, giant 78
Coastline 16
Coati 66
Cobra 26
Cockatiel 47
Cockatoo 44
Colugo 28
Condor, Andean 66, 66
Coniferous forest, *see Forest.*
Coral 78, 78, 79
Cormorant, flightless 69
Cougar 52
Coyote 54, 54
Crab 68, 78
Crane, Manchurian or Japanese 22
Crocodile 39
Cuscus 44, 45

D
Deciduous forest, *see Forest.*
Deep-sea angler 77
Deer 22; fallow 16; mule 52; Pampas 64, 65; red 12, 13; sika 23; white-tailed 56
Deforestation 12, 16, 22, 24, 28, 34, 38, 41, 44, 52, 56, 58, 62
Desert 20, 36, 46
Desman 14
Dingo 47
Dog, dingo 47 raccoon 23; wild 32
Dolphin 77
Domestic animals, competition of wild animals with 20, 46, 48, 54, 64, 68
Dromedary 36, 37
Duck, torrent 66

Dugong 44, 45
Duiker 34

E
Eagle 20, 38; bald 53; golden 15
Echidna, short-beaked 45
Eel 79; electric 62
Elephant, African 32, 33, 34, 38; Asian 27
Elk 20, 22, 53
Emu 47

F
Falcon, prairie 54
Farming 16, 26, 32, 54, 56, 64
Finch 68
Flamingo 39
Forest, bamboo 24; coniferous 12, 14, 20, 22; deciduous 12, 22, 56; eucalyptus 48; rain 28, 34, 44, 58, 62
Fox 56; Arctic 73; fennec 37; red 12
Frog 28

G
Gazelle 32
Gerbil 21
Gharial 27
Giraffe 32, 32
Glider 44, 48
Goat, mountain 52, 53
Gorilla 34; mountain 38, 38
Grassland 32, 54, 64
Guanaco 64
Gull 77

H
Habitat, loss of 12, 14, 16, 22, 26, 34, 44, 58
Hamster 20

Hare 16; European *12*
Hatchet fish 76
Hawk 38; Galápagos *69*
Hedgehog 12, *12*
Heron, great white *57*
Herring 76
Hippopotamus *39*
Hornbill 34
Horse, Przewalski's 20, *21*
Hunting 20, 32, 38, 40, 46, 58,
    68, 72
Hyena 26, *32*
Hyrax 38; tree *38*

I
Ibex 14, *14*; Siberian *24*
Ibis, scarlet *58*
Iguana 58; green *59*; land *69*;
    marine *68*
Island 40, 68

J
Jackal 26
Jackrabbit 54
Jaguar *63*
Jay 12

K
Kakapo 48
Kangaroo 46; gray *49*
Kinkajou *58*
Kiwi 48
Koala 48, *49*

L
Lakes 38
Langur 28; Hanuman *25*
Leopard 34, *35*, 38; clouded *29*;
    snow 24, *25*
Lemming 72
Lemur 40; giant 40; ring-tailed
    41; ruffed *41*
Lily trotter 38
Lion 32, *33*; mountain 52, 56
Lizard, frilled *46*; monitor *36*
Llama 66, *67*

Lorikeet, rainbow *49*
Lynx *15*, 20, 52

M
Macaque 28; Barbary *17*;
    Japanese *23*
Macaw *62*
Mandrill *34*
Mara 64
Margay 58, *59*
Markhor 24
Marmot 14, 24; hoary *52*
Marten, pine 12
Meadowlark 54
Meerkat *36*
Mink 52
Mongoose 26, *40*
Monkey, howler 58, 62;
    proboscis 28; spider 58, 62;
    woolly 58; *see also Langur
    and Macaque.*
Monsoon 22, 26
Moth, silk *25*
Mouflon *17*
Mountains 14, 24, 38, 44, 52,
    58, 66
Mouse 54, 56
Mouselemur, lesser 40
Mudskipper *28*

N
Nightingale 12

O
Ocelot 58, 66
Octopus *76*
Oil, human search for 36, 72
Okapi 34, *35*
Opossum 52, 58
Orang-utan *28*
Oryx, scimitar-horned *37*
Owl, 12, 20; snowy *72*, tawny
    12
Ox, musk 72, *73*
Oxpecker *39*
Oystercatcher 16

P
Panda, giant 24, *25*; red 24
Pangolin *35*
Panther 52
Parakeet *47*
Parrot 34, 44, 58, 62
Peafowl *26*
Peccary, Chacoan *65*
Penguin 72; adelie *73*
Pheasant 24
Pigeon, Victoria crowned *44*
Pika 24
Piranha 62
Plankton 76
Platypus 48, *48*
Poaching 32
Polecat *12*, 20
Pollution 14, 16, 52, 56, 77, 78
Porcupine 52, *52*
Possum 44
Prairie dog 54; black-tailed *55*
Pronghorn *55*
Puffin *73*
Puma 52, *52*

Q
Quetzal *59*

R
Rabbit 12, 14; cottontail *56*
Raccoon *57*
Rain forest, *see Forest.*
Rat, jumping 40
Rattlesnake *55*
Ray, eagle *76*
Reindeer 72, *73*
Rhea *65*
Rhinoceros 38, *39*

S
Sable 20
Saiga 20
Salmon 52
Sandgrouse 36
Sardine 76
Scorpion 37
Seal 72; Mediterranean monk
    16

Shark 76, 77
Sheep, American bighorn 52, 53; Barbary 37
Shrimp 78
Skunk 56
Sloth 63
Spoonbill 16
Squirrel 20, 22, 28, 52, 56; red 13
Starfish 78
Steppe 20
Stork, white 17
Swamps 20, 56, 58

T
Tahr 24
Taiga 20
Tamarin, golden lion 62
Tapir 29, 59
Tarantula 63
Tarsier, Philippine 29
Tasmanian devil 48, 48

Tenrec 40, 41
Tiger 22, 27; Siberian 22
Tortoise, Galápagos 69; giant 40
Toucan 62
Triggerfish 79
Tropical rain forest, see Forest.
Tuatara 48, 49
Tundra 72
Turtle, leatherback 77; loggerhead 16

U
Urchin, sea 78

V
Vicuña 66, 66, 67
Vole 20, 24
Vulture 33; griffon 15

W
Wallaby 46, 48
Warbler 12
Weasel 52
Whale 72, 76, 77
Wildebeest 32
Wisent 13
Wolf 20, 56, 72; maned 64, 64; Tasmanian 48; timber 21
Wolverine 20
Wombat 46, 48; hairy-nosed 46
Woodpecker 12

Y
Yak 25

Z
Zebra 32, 32-33

Index to Major Places on the Maps

Place	Page	Place	Page	Place	Page
Abidjan, Ivory Coast	30	Atacama Desert, Chile	61	Brussels, Belgium	10
Aconcagua, Mount, Argentina	61	Athens, Greece	11	Budapest, Hungary	11
		Atlanta, Georgia	51	Buenos Aires, Argentina	61
Adelaide, Australia	43	Atlantic Ocean	74	Bulgaria (ctry.), Europe	11
Adis Abeba, Ethiopia	31	Atlas Mountains, Africa	30	Burkina Faso (ctry.), Africa	30
Adriatic Sea, Europe	11	Australia (ctry.), Oceania	42	Burma (ctry.), Asia	19
Afghanistan (ctry.), Asia	18	Austria (ctry.), Europe	11	Burundi (ctry.), Africa	31
Ahaggar Mountains, Algeria	31	Baffin Bay, N. Amer.	51	Cairo, Egypt	31
Alaska (state), U.S.	50	Baffin Island, Canada	51	Calcutta, India	19
Alaska, Gulf of, Alaska	50	Baghdad, Iraq	31	Cambodia (ctry.), Asia	19
Alaska Range (mtns.), Alaska	50	Bahamas (ctry.), N. Amer.	51	Cameroon (ctry.), Africa	31
		Baikal, Lake, Soviet Union	19	Canada (ctry.), N. Amer.	51
Albania (ctry.), Europe	11	Baja California (peninsula), Mexico	50	Canberra, Australia	43
Aleutian Islands, Alaska	50			Canton, China	19
Algeria (ctry.), Africa	30	Balearic Islands, Spain	10	Cape York Peninsula, Australia	43
Algiers, Algeria	30	Baltic Sea, Europe	11		
Alice Springs, Australia	43	Bangkok, Thailand	19	Cape Town, South Africa	31
Al-Khartūm, Sudan	31	Bangladesh (ctry.), Asia	19	Caracas, Venezuela	61
Alps (mtns.), Europe	11	Barbados (ctry.), N. Amer.	51	Caribbean Sea	51
Amazon River, S. Amer.	61	Barcelona, Spain	10	Carpathian Mountains, Europe	11
American Highland, Antarctica	71	Barents Sea, Europe	71	Carpentaria, Gulf of, Australia	43
Amsterdam, Netherlands	11	Beaufort Sea, N. Amer.	70		
Amundsen Sea, Antarctica	71	Beijing, China	19	Casablanca, Morocco	30
Amur River, Asia	19	Belém, Brazil	61	Cascade Range (mtns.), N. Amer.	50
Anchorage, Alaska	50	Belgium (ctry.), Europe	11		
Andaman Islands, India	19	Belize (ctry.), N. Amer.	31	Caspian Sea	11
Andes (mtns.), S. Amer.	61	Bengal, Bay of, Asia	19	Caucasus (mtns.), Soviet Union	11
Andorra (ctry.), Europe	10	Benin (ctry.), Africa	30		
Angel Falls, Venezuela	61	Bering Sea	70	Cayman Islands (ctry.), N. Amer.	51
Angola (ctry.), Africa	31	Berlin, Germany	11		
Antarctica (continent)	71	Bhutan (ctry.), Asia	19	Celebes (island), Indonesia	19
Antarctic Peninsula, Antarctica	71	Black Sea	11	Central African Republic (ctry.), Africa	31
		Bogotá, Colombia	61		
Antigua and Barbuda (ctry.), N. Amer.	51	Bolivia (ctry.), S. Amer.	61	Central Russian Uplands, Soviet Union	11
		Bombay, India	3		
Apennines (mtns.), Italy	11	Bonn, Fed. Rep. of Germany	11	Chad (ctry.), Africa	31
Appalachian Mountains, N. Amer.	51			Chad, Lake, Africa	31
		Borneo (island), Asia	19	Chang River, China	19
Arabian Sea	18	Boston, Massachusetts	51	Chengdu, China	19
Arafura Sea	43	Botswana (ctry.), Africa	31	Chicago, Illinois	51
Aral Sea, Soviet Union	18	Brahmaputra River, Asia	19	Chile (ctry.), S. Amer.	61
Arctic Ocean	71	Brasília, Brazil	61	China (ctry.), Asia	19
Argentina (ctry.), S. Amer.	61	Brazil (ctry.), S. Amer.	61	Chongqing, China	19
Arnhem Land (region), Australia	43	Brazilian Highlands, Brazil	61	Cleveland, Ohio	51
		Brisbane, Australia	43	Coast Mountains, N. Amer.	50
Aruba (ctry.), N. Amer.	51	Brooks Range (mtns.), Alaska	50		
Asunción, Paraguay	61	Brunei (ctry.), Asia	19	Coast Ranges (mtns.), U.S.	50

Place	Page	Place	Page	Place	Page
Colombia (ctry.), S. Amer.	61	Finland (ctry.), Europe	11	Guyana (ctry.), S. Amer.	61
Columbia River, N. Amer.	50	Fortaleza, Brazil	61		
Congo (ctry.), Africa	31	France (ctry.), Europe	10	Haiti (ctry.), N. Amer.	51
Congo Basin, Africa	31	French Guiana (ctry.), S.		Hamburg, Fed. Rep. of	
Congo River, Africa	31	Amer.	61	Germany	11
Copenhagen, Denmark	11			Havana, Cuba	51
Coral Sea, Oceania	43	Gabon (ctry.), Africa	31	Helsinki, Finland	11
Córdoba, Argentina	61	Galápagos Islands,		Himalayas (mtns.), Asia	19
Corsica (island), France	11	Ecuador	60	Hobart, Australia	43
Costa Rica (ctry.), N.		Gambia (ctry.), Africa	30	Honduras (ctry.), N.	
Amer.	51	Ganges River, Asia	19	Amer.	51
Crete (island), Greece	11	German Democratic		Hong Kong (ctry.), Asia	19
Cuba (ctry.), N. Amer.	51	Republic (ctry.), Europe	11	Horn, Cape, Chile	61
Czechoslovakia (ctry.),		Germany, Federal		Houston, Texas	51
Europe	11	Republic of (ctry.),		Huang River, China	19
		Europe	11	Hudson Bay, Canada	51
Dakar, Senegal	30	Ghana (ctry.), Africa	30	Hungary (ctry.), Europe	11
Dallas, Texas	51	Gibraltar (ctry.), Europe	10	Huron, Lake, N. Amer.	51
Danube River, Europe	11	Gibson Desert, Australia	42		
Dar es Salaam, Tanzania	31	Gobi (desert), Asia	19	Iceland (ctry.), Europe	10
Darling River, Australia	43	Gran Chaco (plain), S.		Iguaçu Falls, S. Amer.	61
Darwin, Australia	42	Amer.	61	India (ctry.), Asia	19
Deccan (plateau), India	19	Grande, Rio (r.), N. Amer.	51	Indian Ocean	75
Delhi, India	19	Great Australian Bight		Indonesia (ctry.), Asia	19
Denmark (ctry.), Europe	11	(bay), Australia	42	Indus River, Asia	19
Denver, Colorado	51	Great Barrier Reef,		Ireland (ctry.), Europe	10
Detroit, Michigan	51	Australia	43	Irrawaddy River, Burma	19
Dominica (ctry.), N. Amer.	51	Great Basin, U.S.	50	Istanbul, Turkey	11
Dominican Republic		Great Bear Lake, Canada	50	Italy (ctry.), Europe	11
(ctry.), N. Amer.	51	Great Dividing Range		Ivory Coast (ctry.), Africa	30
Don River, Soviet Union	11	(mtns.), Australia	43		
Djibouti (ctry.), Africa	31	Great Lakes, N. Amer.	74	Jakarta, Indonesia	19
		Great Plains, N. Amer.	51	Jamaica (ctry.), N. Amer.	51
East China Sea, Asia	19	Great Salt Lake, Utah	50	Japan (ctry.), Asia	19
Ecuador (ctry.), S. Amer.	61	Great Sandy Desert,		Japan, Sea of, Asia	19
Edinburgh, Scotland	10	Australia	42	Java (island), Indonesia	19
Edmonton, Alberta	50	Great Slave Lake, Canada	51		
Egypt (ctry.), Africa	31	Great Victoria Desert,		Kalahari Desert, Africa	31
El Salvador (ctry.), N.		Australia	42	Karāchi, Pakistan	18
Amer.	51	Greece (ctry.), Europe	11	Kenya (ctry.), Africa	31
Equatorial Guinea (ctry.),		Greenland (ctry.), N.		Kiev, Soviet Union	11
Africa	31	Amer.	2	Kilimanjaro, Mount,	
Erie, Lake, N. Amer.	51	Grenada (ctry.), N. Amer.	51	Tanzania	31
Ethiopia (ctry.), Africa	31	Guadeloupe (ctry.), N.		Kinshasa, Zaire	31
Everest, Mount, Asia	19	Amer.	51		
Eyre, Lake, Australia	43	Guatemala (ctry.), N.		Labrador Sea, N. Amer.	51
		Amer.	51	Ladoga, Lake, Soviet	
Faeroe Islands (ctry.),		Guiana Highlands, S.		Union	11
Europe	10	Amer.	61	Lagos, Nigeria	30
Falkland Islands (ctry.), S.		Guinea (ctry.), Africa	30	Laos (ctry.), Asia	19
Amer.	61	Guinea-Bissau (ctry.),		La Paz, Bolivia	61
Fiji (ctry.), Oceania	43	Africa	30	Lena River, Soviet Union	70

Place	Page	Place	Page	Place	Page
Leningrad, Soviet Union	11	Missouri River, U.S.	51	North Sea, Europe	11
Lesotho (ctry.), Africa	31	Mongolia (ctry.), Asia	19	Norway (ctry.), Europe	11
Lhasa, China	19	Monterrey, Mexico	51	Norwegian Sea, Europe	71
Liberia (ctry.), Africa	30	Montevideo, Uruguay	61	Nyasa, Lake, Africa	31
Libya (ctry.), Africa	31	Montréal, Quebec	51		
Liechtenstein (ctry.), Europe	11	Montserrat (ctry.), N. Amer.	51	Ob River, Soviet Union	71
Lima, Peru	61	Morocco (ctry.), Africa	30	Ohio River, U.S.	51
Limpopo River, Africa	31	Moscow, Soviet Union	11	Okavango River, Africa	31
Lisbon, Portugal	10	Mozambique (ctry.), Africa	31	Okhotsk, Sea of, Asia	70
Llanos (plain), S. Amer.	61	Mozambique Channel, Africa	31	Onega, Lake, Soviet Union	11
London, England	10	Munich, Fed. Rep. of Germany	11	Ontario, Lake, N. Amer.	51
Los Angeles, California	50	Murray River, Australia	43	Orinoco River, S. Amer.	61
Luxembourg (ctry.), Europe	11			Oslo, Norway	11
		Nairobi, Kenya	31	Pacific Ocean	74
Macdonnell Ranges (mtns.), Australia	42	Namib Desert, Namibia	31	Pakistan (ctry.), Asia	19
Mackenzie Mountains, Canada	50	Namibia (ctry.), Africa	31	Pampa (plain), Argentina	61
Mackenzie River, Canada	50	Nanjing, China	19	Panama (ctry.), N. Amer.	51
Madagascar (ctry.), Africa	31	Nasser, Lake, Africa	31	Papua New Guinea (ctry.), Oceania	43
Madre, Sierra (mtns.), Mexico	51	Nepal (ctry.), Asia	19	Paraguay (ctry.), S. Amer.	61
Madrid, Spain	10	Netherlands (ctry.), Europe	11	Paraguay River, S. Amer.	61
Malawi (ctry.), Africa	31	Netherlands Antilles (islands), N. Amer.	51	Paraná River, S. Amer.	61
Malaysia (ctry.), Asia	19	Nevada, Sierra (mtns.), U.S.	50	Paris, France	10
Mali (ctry.), Africa	30	New Caledonia (island), Oceania	43	Patagonia (region), Argentina	61
Malta (ctry.), Europe	11	Newfoundland (island), Canada	51	Perth, Australia	42
Managua, Nicaragua	51	New Guinea (island)	43	Peru (ctry.), S. Amer.	61
Manaus, Brazil	61	New Hebrides (islands), Oceania	43	Philadelphia, Pennsylvania	51
Manchester, England	10	New York, New York	51	Philippines (ctry.), Asia	19
Manchuria (region), China	19	New Zealand (ctry.), Oceania	43	Plata, Río de la (bay), S. Amer.	61
Manila, Philippines	19	Nicaragua (ctry.), N. Amer.	51	Poland (ctry.), Europe	11
Maracaibo, Lake, Venezuela	61	Nicaragua, Lake, Nicaragua	51	Port Moresby, Papua New Guinea	43
Martinique (ctry.), N. Amer.	51	Niger (ctry.), Africa	31	Portugal (ctry.), Europe	10
Mato Grosso Plateau, Brazil	61	Nigeria (ctry.), Africa	31	Pretoria, South Africa	31
Mauritania (ctry.), Africa	30	Niger River, Africa	31	Puerto Rico (ctry.), N. Amer.	51
McKinley, Mount, Alaska	50	Nile River, Africa	31	Pyrenees (mtns.), Europe	10
Mediterranean Sea	31	North European Plain, Europe	11		
Mekong River, Asia	19	North Island, New Zealand	43	Queen Elizabeth Islands, Canada	51
Melbourne, Australia	43	North Korea (ctry.), Asia	19	Quito, Ecuador	61
Mexico (ctry.), N. Amer.	51	North Pole	71		
Mexico City, Mexico	51			Red Sea	31
Mexico, Gulf of, N. Amer.	51			Rhine River, Europe	11
Miami, Florida	51			Rhone River, Europe	11
Michigan, Lake, U.S.	51			Rift Valley, Africa	31
Milan, Italy	10			Rio de Janeiro, Brazil	61
Mississippi River, U.S.	51				

INDEX TO MAJOR PLACES ON THE MAPS   93

Place	Page	Place	Page	Place	Page
Rocky Mountains, N. Amer.	50	Sri Lanka (ctry.), Asia	19	Ubangi River, Africa	31
Romania (ctry.), Europe	11	St. Louis, Missouri	51	Uganda (ctry.), Africa	31
Rome, Italy	11	Stockholm, Sweden	11	United Kingdom (ctry.), Europe	10
Ross Ice Shelf, Antarctica	71	Sudan (ctry.), Africa	31	United States (ctry.), N. Amer.	51
Ross Sea, Antarctica	71	Sudan (region), Africa	31	Ural Mountains, Soviet Union	11
Rudolf, Lake, Africa	31	Sumatra (island), Indonesia	19	Ural River, Soviet Union	11
Ruwenzori Range (mtns.), Africa	31	Superior, Lake, N. Amer.	51	Uruguay (ctry.), S. Amer.	61
Rwanda (ctry.), Africa	31	Suriname (ctry.), S. Amer.	61		
		Svalbard (islands), Europe	71	Vancouver, British Columbia	50
Sahara (desert), Africa	31	Swaziland (ctry.), Africa	31	Vanern, Lake, Sweden	11
Saint Lawrence River, N. Amer.	51	Sweden (ctry.), Europe	11	Vanuatu (ctry.), Oceania	43
Saint Lucia (ctry.), N. Amer.	51	Switzerland (ctry.), Europe	11	Vattern, Lake, Sweden	11
		Sydney, Australia	43	Venezuela (ctry.), S. Amer.	61
		Szechwan Basin, China	19	Victoria Falls, Africa	31
Saint Vincent and the Grenadines (ctry.), N. Amer.	51	T'aipei, Taiwan	19	Victoria Island, Canada	51
San Francisco, California	50	Taiwan (ctry.), Asia	19	Victoria, Lake, Africa	31
Santiago, Chile	61	Tanganyika, Lake, Africa	31	Vienna, Austria	11
São Paulo, Brazil	61	Tanzania (ctry.), Africa	31	Vietnam (ctry.), Asia	19
Sao Tome and Principe (ctry.), Africa	31	Tapajós River, Brazil	61	Virgin Islands, N. Amer.	51
Sardinia (island), Italy	11	Tarim Basin, China	19	Volga River, Soviet Union	11
Saskatchewan River, Canada	51	Taškent, Soviet Union	19	Volgograd, Soviet Union	11
Seattle, Washington	50	Tasmania (island), Australia	43		
Selvas (forest), Brazil	61	Tasman Sea, Oceania	43	Warsaw, Poland	11
Senegal (ctry.), Africa	30	Tegucigalpa, Honduras	51	Washington, Dist. of Columbia	51
Serengeti Plain, Tanzania	31	Tehrān, Iran	31	Weddell Sea, Antarctica	71
Shanghai, China	19	Thailand (ctry.), Asia	19	Wellington, New Zealand	43
Shenyang, China	19	The Everglades (swamp), U.S.	51	Western Sahara (ctry.), Africa	30
Siberia (region), Soviet Union	19	Tibet, Plateau of, China	19	West Indies (islands)	51
Sicily (island), Italy	11	Tien Shan (mtns.), Asia	19	Winnipeg, Lake, Canada	51
Sierra Leone (ctry.), Africa	30	Timbuktu, Mali	30	Wuhan, China	19
Singapore (ctry.), Asia	19	Timor (island), Indonesia	42		
Solomon Islands (ctry.), Oceania	43	Titicaca, Lake, S. Amer.	61	Xi'an, China	19
Somalia (ctry.), Africa	31	Togo (ctry.), Africa	30		
Sŏul, South Korea	19	Tōkyō, Japan	19	Yellow Sea, Asia	19
South Africa (ctry.), Africa	31	Tonga (ctry.), Oceania	43	Yucatan Peninsula, N. Amer.	51
South China Sea, Asia	19	Toronto, Ontario	51	Yugoslavia (ctry.), Europe	11
Southern Ocean	75	Torres Strait, Oceania	43	Yukon River, N. Amer.	50
South Island, New Zealand	43	Transantarctic Mountains, Antarctica	71		
South Korea (ctry.), Asia	19	Trinidad and Tobago (ctry.), N. Amer.	51	Zaire (ctry.), Africa	31
Soviet Union (ctry.)	11	Tripoli, Libya	31	Zambezi River, Africa	31
Spain (ctry.), Europe	10	Tunisia (ctry.), Africa	31	Zambia (ctry.), Africa	31
		Turkey (ctry.)	11	Zimbabwe (ctry.), Africa	31
		Tuvalu (ctry.), Oceania	43